Quilts by Adrienne Yorinks

❖

Written by Adrienne Yorinks and
50 Librarians From Across the Nation

❖

Librarian contributions compiled and edited
by Jeanette Larson

NATIONAL GEOGRAPHIC
WASHINGTON, D.C.

*This book is dedicated to
my brother and sister.*

Many thanks to:

• My dear friend and Librarian Extraordinaire, Jeanette Larson, who helped in so many ways. Her excitement about the project from the beginning, her finding 49 other librarians so there would be one for each state, her wonderful text on Texas, and the time we spent in Texas talking about the project have all been vital to creating *Quilt of States*.

• The 50 librarians for their efforts in making this book so special.

• The wonderful staff at National Geographic for their vision and faith in the project: Nancy Feresten, who has been involved from the beginning; Marfé Ferguson Delano; my editor, Susan Donnelly; art director, Bea Jackson, and the photography staff who worked so hard to capture the intricacies of this art.

• Suzan Ellis, who created "The State Flower Fabrics" for Northcott Monarch and, generously gave me a half yard of each to incorporate into the textile art for each state. These fabrics are available in her catalog, *Quilts and Other Comforts*, or her website at www.quiltsonline.com. You can use them to create your own state quilt.

• Emily Cohen, from Timeless Treasures, who sent me some wonderful conversational prints to use, and Suzanne Sunday and Therese Barkley, quiltmakers and friends who shared some fabric from their own stashes for this book.

• All textile artists who created the fabrics used in this book.

• Linda Douglas and Pat Kole of the Idaho Potato Commission for allowing us to use Spuddy Buddy for the state of Idaho.

• I also wish to thank Jerry Berg; Helene Berg; Steven, Elise, Meredith, Matthew, and Mark Berg; Nancy, Barry, Sarah, and Daniel Troy; and Leatrice, Benjamin, and Sophie Schoenberg for all their support. My husband, Douglas Schoenberg, whose knowledge of history astounds me and who patiently read the manuscript and offered advice.

• And a special thanks to Harry and La Redda, my red poodles, for spending every hour with me in both writing and illustrating this book and who always tell me everything I do is fabulous!

Published by the National Geographic Society.

Book design by Susan Kehnemui Donnelly.

The body text of the book is set in Hoefler New.
The display text is set in Carmilla, Cochin-Archaic, and P22 Folk Art.

Printed in China.

Library of Congress Cataloging-in-Publication Data

Yorinks, Adrienne.
  Quilt of states / written by Adrienne Yorinks and fifty librarians from across the United States ; illustrated by Adrienne Yorinks. p. cm.
  1. U.S. states—History—Juvenile literature. 2. United States—History—Colonial period, ca. 1600-1775—Juvenile literature. 3. Statehood (American politics)—History—Juvenile literature. I. Title.
  E180.Y67 2005
  973—dc22

              2004017796

Hardcover ISBN: 0-7922-7285-4
Library Edition ISBN: 0-7922-7286-2

One of the world's largest nonprofit scientific and educational organizations, the National Geographic Society was founded in 1888 "for the increase and diffusion of geographic knowledge." Fulfilling this mission, the Society educates and inspires millions every day through its magazines, books, television programs, videos, maps and atlases, research grants, the National Geographic Bee, teacher workshops, and innovative classroom materials. The Society is supported through membership dues, charitable gifts, and income from the sale of its educational products. This support is vital to National Geographic's mission to increase global understanding and promote conservation of our planet through exploration, research, and education.

For more information, please call 1-800-NGS-LINE (647-5463) or write to the following address:

NATIONAL GEOGRAPHIC SOCIETY
1145 17th Street N.W.
Washington, D.C. 20036-4688

Visit the Society's Web site:
www.nationalgeographic.com

Table of Contents

"The Constitution gives Congress the power to admit new states
to the Union (Article IV, Section 3). The procedure itself involves
the following steps: Congress must first receive a petition for statehood from the
legislature of the territory or independent state. If Congress approves the petition,
the legislature then must draft a proposed state constitution.
Once Congress has accepted the constitution, it can then enact a bill
to admit the state. But statehood does not actually become
official until the president has signed the bill into law."

– Congressional Quarterly's *Desk Reference on the States*

A Historical Introduction

WHEN EUROPEANS FIRST CAME TO THE AMERICAS, they thought they had discovered empty, uncharted territory. But Native Americans and their ancestors had populated the land for centuries. The many different tribes lived in many different ways and held diverse cultural and political points of view, but they all shared one common harsh fate: They were subjected to slavery, disease, warfare, and later even forced removal when the Europeans settled the land.

By the mid-1650s, Spanish, British, Dutch, and French settlements had been established throughout North America. As the years passed, Britain became a superpower. It controlled territories around the world, including the 13 Colonies that formed the core of the original U.S., as well as most of what is now eastern Canada. By the mid-1700s, the Colonies were a cultured, successful civilization.

In 1754 Britain owed huge debts from the Seven Years War (which included the French and Indian War in North America) and began taxing the Colonies to pay its bills. Anti-British sentiment began to grow in the Colonies. In 1774 representatives from the colonies came together at a Continental Congress to discuss the problem, and fighting broke out in Massachusetts in the spring of 1775.

American patriots—with help from France—defeated the British in 1781. With the Treaty of Versailles in 1783, Britain recognized the now former Colonies as independent. Representatives drew up the Articles of Confederation, an attempt to establish a national government. Some thought that the articles were too weak to work well. In 1787 they created a structure for our national government—the Constitution.

Each colony would need to ratify, or accept, the Constitution to become a state. Not all colonists were pleased with the new document, and there was some resistance. But eventually, all 13 former Colonies ratified the Constitution and joined a new nation. It would take more than 170 years from the creation of the first state for the U.S. to become the 50 states that it is today. Every state has had its own unique path to statehood. This is their story.

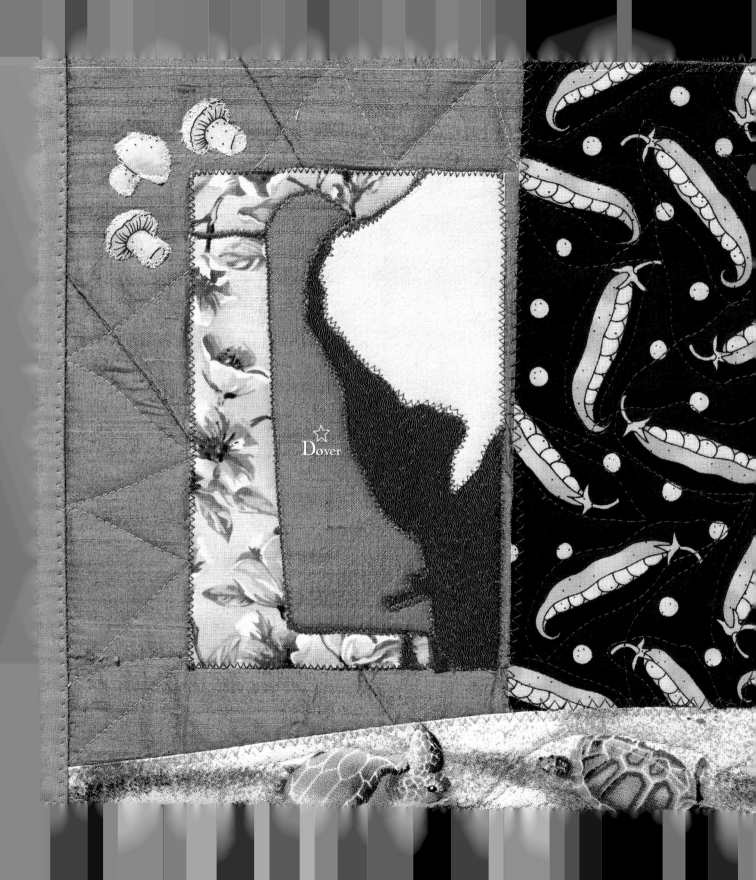

Dover

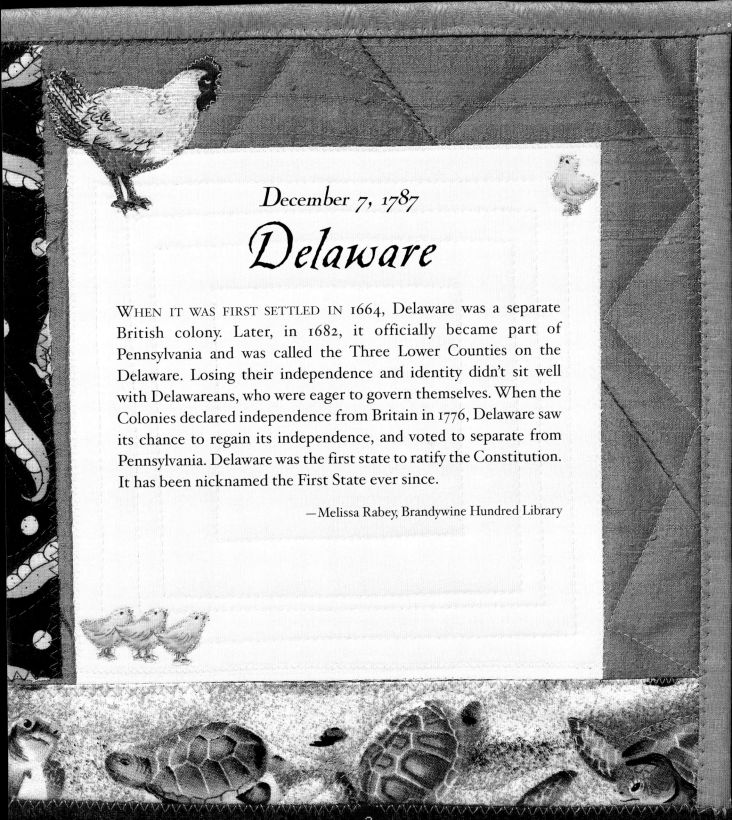

December 7, 1787
Delaware

WHEN IT WAS FIRST SETTLED IN 1664, Delaware was a separate British colony. Later, in 1682, it officially became part of Pennsylvania and was called the Three Lower Counties on the Delaware. Losing their independence and identity didn't sit well with Delawareans, who were eager to govern themselves. When the Colonies declared independence from Britain in 1776, Delaware saw its chance to regain its independence, and voted to separate from Pennsylvania. Delaware was the first state to ratify the Constitution. It has been nicknamed the First State ever since.

—Melissa Rabey, Brandywine Hundred Library

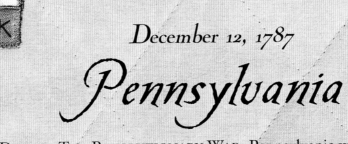

December 12, 1787

Pennsylvania

DURING THE REVOLUTIONARY WAR, Pennsylvania was the link joining the militant northern colonies and the more conservative southern colonies in their struggle for freedom. After winning their independence, the former colonies were still divided on how the new national government should be organized. In 1787 a Constitutional Convention was held in Philadelphia, Pennsylvania. Delegate Gouverneur Morris compiled all of the resolutions and decisions of the convention into a polished document. He is often credited with "writing" the Constitution. Pennsylvania's ratification of the Constitution ensured its statehood. Like Virginia, Massachusetts, and Kentucky, Pennsylvania is technically a commonwealth—meaning "public good." From 1790 to 1800, Philadelphia served as the capital of the new nation.

—Lynn Moses, Pennsylvania Department of Education

★ Harrisburg

★ Trenton

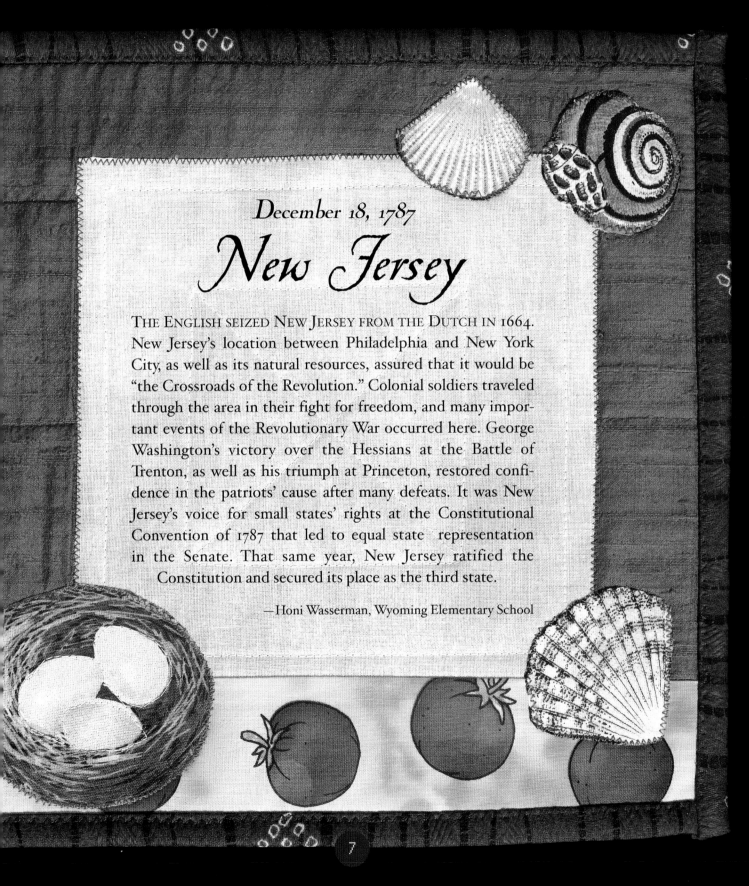

December 18, 1787

New Jersey

THE ENGLISH SEIZED NEW JERSEY FROM THE DUTCH IN 1664. New Jersey's location between Philadelphia and New York City, as well as its natural resources, assured that it would be "the Crossroads of the Revolution." Colonial soldiers traveled through the area in their fight for freedom, and many important events of the Revolutionary War occurred here. George Washington's victory over the Hessians at the Battle of Trenton, as well as his triumph at Princeton, restored confidence in the patriots' cause after many defeats. It was New Jersey's voice for small states' rights at the Constitutional Convention of 1787 that led to equal state representation in the Senate. That same year, New Jersey ratified the Constitution and secured its place as the third state.

—Honi Wasserman, Wyoming Elementary School

☆ **Atlanta**

GEORGIA
PEACHES
FRESHLY PICKED
CAREFULLY PRESERV

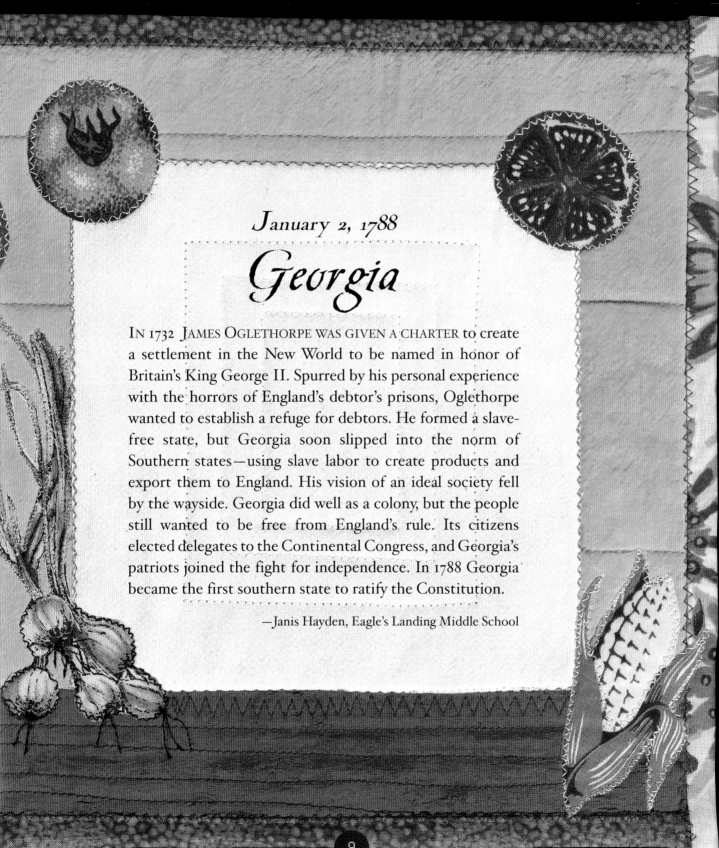

January 2, 1788

Georgia

IN 1732 JAMES OGLETHORPE WAS GIVEN A CHARTER to create a settlement in the New World to be named in honor of Britain's King George II. Spurred by his personal experience with the horrors of England's debtor's prisons, Oglethorpe wanted to establish a refuge for debtors. He formed a slave-free state, but Georgia soon slipped into the norm of Southern states—using slave labor to create products and export them to England. His vision of an ideal society fell by the wayside. Georgia did well as a colony, but the people still wanted to be free from England's rule. Its citizens elected delegates to the Continental Congress, and Georgia's patriots joined the fight for independence. In 1788 Georgia became the first southern state to ratify the Constitution.

—Janis Hayden, Eagle's Landing Middle School

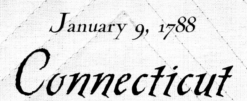

January 9, 1788

Connecticut

EVEN EARLY ON, COLONISTS OF CONNECTICUT wanted to decide their own style of government and way of life independent from British rule. In 1639 they wrote the Fundamental Orders, a document that talked of a government "by the people." It created a society governed by the rule of law with a distinct system of representation. Some claim this document was the first written constitution for a democratic government, and Connecticut came to be called "Constitution State." Following the Treaty of Paris in 1783 and ratification of the Constitution, Connecticut became the nation's fifth state.

—Veronica Stevenson-Moudamane, Danbury Library

☆ Hartford

February 6, 1788
Massachusetts

IN 1620 A GROUP OF PURITAN ENGLISH MEN AND WOMEN came to the New World and established Plymouth Colony. In 1691 Britain united Plymouth Colony with its neighbor Massachusetts Bay Colony. The colonists were outraged when England started increasing their taxes. After the French and Indian War, Massachusetts, especially Boston, became a center of rebellion against British rule. As the Revolutionary War began in 1775, Massachusetts was the scene of Paul Revere's ride to warn the Minutemen, the Battles of Lexington and Concord, and the Battle of Bunker Hill. When the Declaration of Independence was written, delegate John Hancock of Massachusetts was the first to sign. Five years after the end of the Revolutionary War, Massachusetts ratified the Constitution and became a state.

—Mary Ann Tourjee, Central Massachusetts Regional Library System

Boston ☆

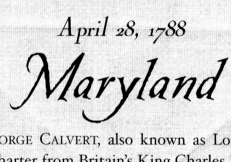

April 28, 1788

Maryland

IN 1623 GEORGE CALVERT, also known as Lord Baltimore, received a charter from Britain's King Charles I for a colony, which he named "Avalon." There, Catholics like him would be free to practice their religion. After Calvert's death, his son, Cecilius Calvert, established the new colony, but named it Maryland in honor of Henrietta Marie, wife of Charles I. From 1763 to 1767, a boundary between Maryland and Pennsylvania—the Mason-Dixon Line—was established. It served as a dividing line between the free states of the North and the slave states of the South. In 1788 following the Revolutionary War, Maryland, one of the original 13 Colonies, gained statehood. Maryland's allegiance to its country was proved in 1791 when the state gave part of its land to the Federal government for a national capital that eventually became the District of Columbia.

—Stacy Brown, Judith Resnik Elementary School

☆ Annapolis

May 23, 1788
South Carolina

IN THE EARLY 1700S the port of Charles Towne (now Charleston) was one of North America's busiest ports. The state imported manufactured goods and exported rice and other products to Britain. Charles Towne also served as a port for slave trading, bringing in workers for the many plantations in the region. South Carolina became a prosperous colony because of its growing economy and port. As America faced the Revolutionary War, South Carolinians were divided in their loyalties. At first, the state's delegates to the Continental Congress voted against the Declaration of Independence, but they changed their vote after hearing that the British had attacked Charles Towne. On May 23, 1788, South Carolina became the eighth state.

—Tammy Williams, Greenwood County Library

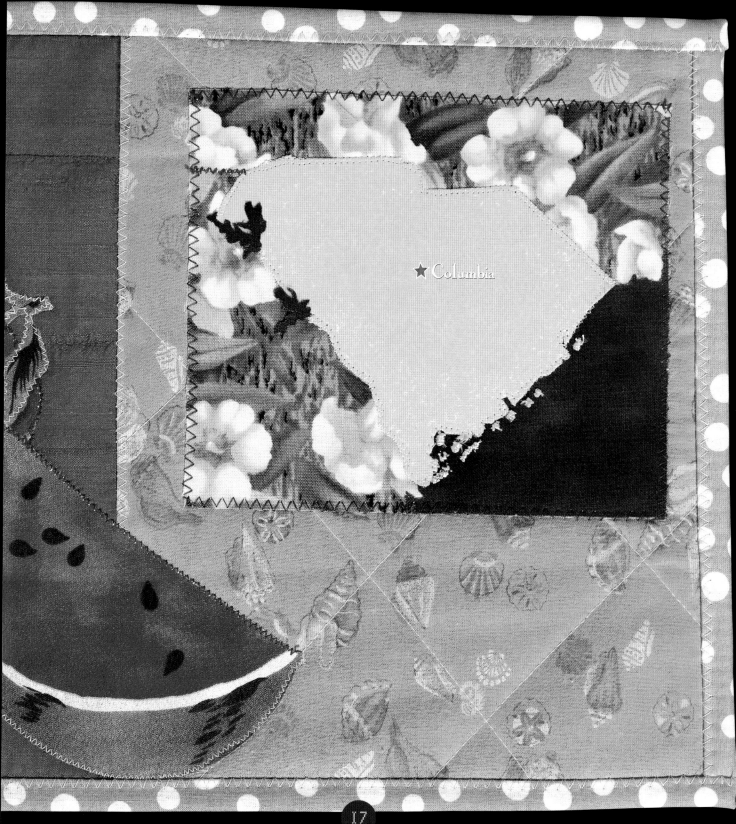

★ Columbia

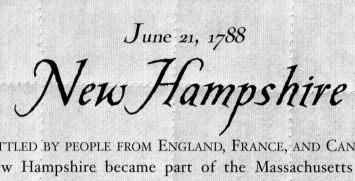

June 21, 1788
New Hampshire

SETTLED BY PEOPLE FROM ENGLAND, FRANCE, AND CANADA, New Hampshire became part of the Massachusetts Bay Colony in 1641. After almost 150 years as part of Massachusetts, New Hampshire became a separate colony, adopting its own constitution on January 5, 1776. Almost six months later, the U.S. Declaration of Independence was signed. Always a haven for freedom seekers, as shown by the state slogan, "Live Free or Die," New Hampshire was eager to join the Union. The Constitution needed only nine of the original 13 Colonies to ratify it in order to make it law for the newly forming country. When New Hampshire ratified the Constitution in 1788, it became the ninth state and made the Constitution the law of the land.

—Ann Hoey, New Hampshire State Library

☆Concord

Richmond ☆

June 25, 1788

Virginia

JAMESTOWN, VIRGINIA, WAS THE FIRST PERMANENT BRITISH colony in the New World. Initially a private enterprise, Virginia became England's first royal colony in the New World in 1624. Having long been under the thumb of British rule, many Virginians were pleased when the Declaration of Independence gave voice to their wish to govern themselves. Although the Constitution had enough votes from other states for ratification, the new government needed the support of the largest and most populated state—Virginia—to succeed. Today, the state is often called the "Mother of States" because large portions of the land that originally made up the colony became all or part of several other states, including West Virginia, Ohio, and Kentucky.

—Julie Dasso, Fairfax County Public Library

July 26, 1788
New York

NEW YORK STATE'S GEOGRAPHY—harbors, mountains, farmland, and waterways—attracted settlers from diverse cultures. In 1624 30 families journeyed from Holland to the land they called New Netherland. The Dutch purchased Manhattan Island (later renamed New Amsterdam) from the native population in 1626 for goods worth 60 Dutch guilders ($24). Almost 40 years later, in 1664, the English Duke of York sent warships to conquer the Dutch, and New Amsterdam became New York City. After the Revolutionary War, many New Yorkers worried that a strong central government for the new nation would take away their rights. They were reluctant to ratify the Constitution. In the end, the delegates argued for more than a month before they heeded the example set by other colonies and agreed to accept the Constitution and join the new nation.

—Starr LaTronica, Four County Library System

Albany ★

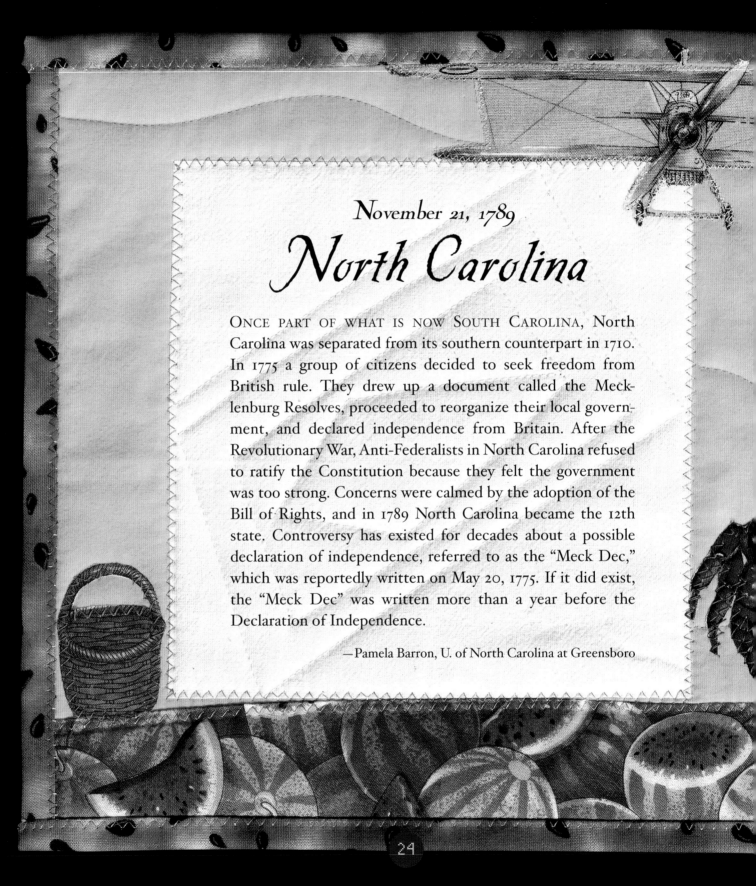

November 21, 1789

North Carolina

ONCE PART OF WHAT IS NOW SOUTH CAROLINA, North Carolina was separated from its southern counterpart in 1710. In 1775 a group of citizens decided to seek freedom from British rule. They drew up a document called the Mecklenburg Resolves, proceeded to reorganize their local government, and declared independence from Britain. After the Revolutionary War, Anti-Federalists in North Carolina refused to ratify the Constitution because they felt the government was too strong. Concerns were calmed by the adoption of the Bill of Rights, and in 1789 North Carolina became the 12th state. Controversy has existed for decades about a possible declaration of independence, referred to as the "Meck Dec," which was reportedly written on May 20, 1775. If it did exist, the "Meck Dec" was written more than a year before the Declaration of Independence.

—Pamela Barron, U. of North Carolina at Greensboro

☆ Raleigh

☆ Providence

May 29, 1790

Rhode Island

AFTER BEING THROWN OUT OF THE MASSACHUSETTS BAY Colony because they disagreed with the beliefs of its Puritan leaders, the first European settlers in Rhode Island bought land from the Narragansett Indians in 1636. On May 4, 1776, two months before any of the other 12 colonies did so, rebellious Rhode Island became the first of the original colonies to declare independence from the British. Despite this, the state was the last of the 13 Colonies to sign the Constitution. Rhode Islanders feared that the larger states, with more people and more votes, would overpower their independence as a small state if a national government existed. The state wanted the U.S. to adopt the first ten amendments to the Constitution—the Bill of Rights—before it would join, as it would help to ensure that their freedoms were protected.

—Carin Steger Kaag, Lawnton Elementary School

The United States in 1790

By 1790 all of the original Colonies had ratified the Constitution. What had been a group of 13 independent countries under the Articles of Confederation came together as one.

The capital was moved to Philadelphia, and George Washington took the helm as the nation's first President. Through the courage and perseverance of many, 13 rebel colonies had pieced themselves together as a national quilt of states.

Established states

Territories won in the Revolution

Spanish possessions

Claimed by the U.S.

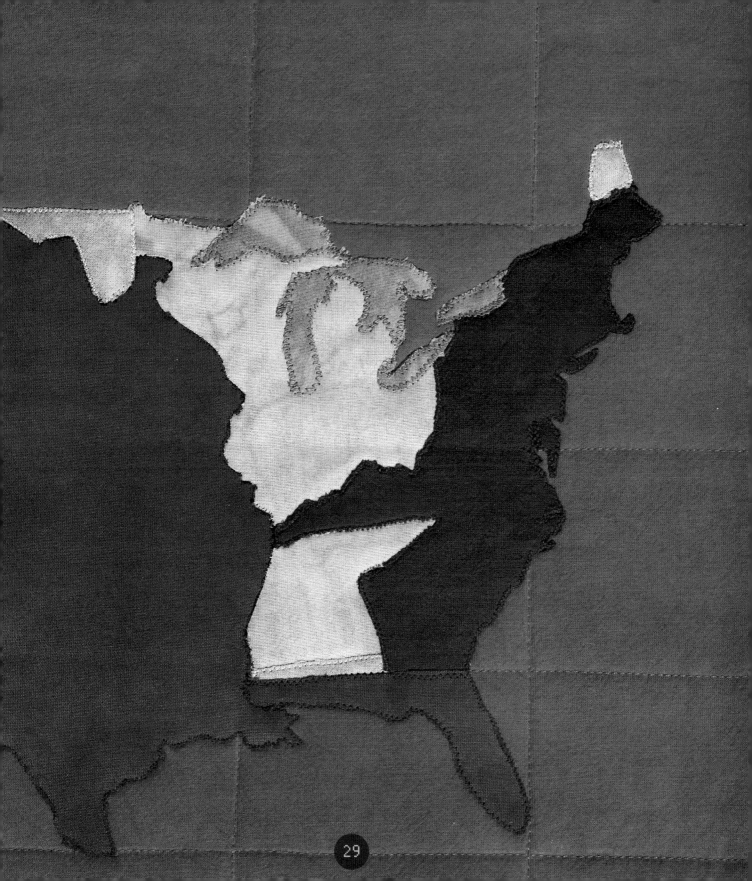

29

March 4, 1791
Vermont

CLAIMED AT TIMES BY BOTH New York and New Hampshire, Vermont was never a separate colony of its own. In January 1777, after the Revolutionary War began, Vermont chose to become an independent republic—its own country. In July of the same year, the country of Vermont adopted a constitution that outlawed slavery and gave voting rights to all adult males, regardless of race, religion, or land ownership. This was a very unusual occurrence. Men who did not own property had never before been given the right to vote. In 1791 after four years as an independent country, Vermont adopted the United States Constitution, and Congress admitted it as the 14th state.

—Grace Worcester Greene, Vermont Department of Libraries

Montpelier

★ Frankfort

June 1, 1792

Kentucky

DEFYING THE BRITISH PROCLAMATION that forbade settlement west of the Appalachians, hunters and explorers made their way to the region in the mid-1770s. When the Revolutionary War ended, the area became a western county of Virginia, which was supposed to protect it. But Kentuckians did not feel a part of Virginia and thought that the state was not upholding its responsibility. They wanted more freedom. Some wanted to be a state of the new U.S., while others sought independence as a new nation. Because Spain owned the land west of the Mississippi and controlled trade down the Mississippi River, some even considered an alliance with Spain. Ultimately, ties to the new nation won out. Kentucky became the first state west of the Appalachians.

—James C. Klotter, State Historian

☆ Nashville

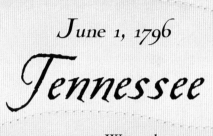

June 1, 1796

Tennessee

AFTER THE REVOLUTIONARY WAR, the states were required to pay a war debt to the federal government. As part of North Carolina at the time, Tennessee was given to the United States as payment of part of the war debt for North Carolina. Feeling that they had no voice in the government, Tennessee settlers decided to organize their own government. Between 1784 and 1787, they formed their own country called Franklin (after Benjamin Franklin). They wrote a constitution, elected a governor, and even coined money. The state disbanded in 1788. Eight years later, on June 1, 1796, Tennessee became the 16th state.

— Karen McIntyre, Westmeade Elementary School

March 1, 1803
Ohio

THE STORY OF OHIO'S STATEHOOD DATES FROM 1787, with the creation of the Northwest Territory, an area later divided into more than five individual states. Ohio was the first state to be established from this vast territory. It was also the first that had to meet the new requirements for any state wishing to join the Union. Each territory must have a governor and a population of at least 60,000 people in order to become a state. In Ohio, the population was large, and a governor was elected, so it was eligible for statehood. But the story does not end there. The Congressional custom for formally declaring a state did not begin until 1812, nine years after Ohio became a state, with the admission of Louisiana. On the eve of the 1953 Ohio sesquicentennial, this oversight was discovered. President Dwight Eisenhower signed legislation retroactively declaring March 1, 1803, the formal date Ohio was admitted to the Union.

—Sue McCleaf Nespeca, Kid Lit Plus Consulting, Youngstown

☆ Columbus

The Louisiana Purchase, 1803

In May 1803 the United States, on the suggestion of President Thomas Jefferson, bought the vast stretch of territory west of the Mississippi River to the Rocky Mountains. This area was known as the Louisiana Purchase. The land, once owned by Spain, was bought from Napoleon Bonaparte, the Emperor of France. The purchase cost 15 million dollars, approximately four cents an acre. This was one of the best land bargains ever—doubling the size of the United States.

Fifteen of today's 50 states were carved out of the Louisiana Purchase territory. The purchase gave the United States control of the Mississippi River, a crucial commercial waterway. It was Jefferson's bold purchase that began the piecing together of what would become a continent-spanning nation, an even broader quilt of states.

Established states

Territories

Louisiana Purchase

Spanish possessions

British possessions

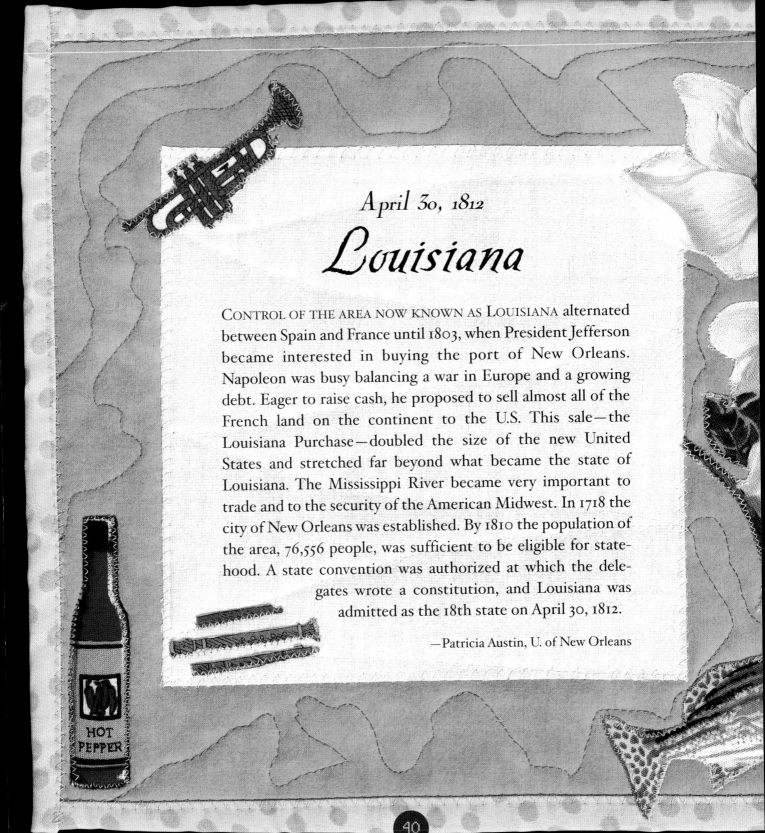

April 30, 1812

Louisiana

CONTROL OF THE AREA NOW KNOWN AS LOUISIANA alternated between Spain and France until 1803, when President Jefferson became interested in buying the port of New Orleans. Napoleon was busy balancing a war in Europe and a growing debt. Eager to raise cash, he proposed to sell almost all of the French land on the continent to the U.S. This sale—the Louisiana Purchase—doubled the size of the new United States and stretched far beyond what became the state of Louisiana. The Mississippi River became very important to trade and to the security of the American Midwest. In 1718 the city of New Orleans was established. By 1810 the population of the area, 76,556 people, was sufficient to be eligible for statehood. A state convention was authorized at which the delegates wrote a constitution, and Louisiana was admitted as the 18th state on April 30, 1812.

—Patricia Austin, U. of New Orleans

HOT PEPPER

Baton Rouge

Indianapolis

December 11, 1816

Indiana

WHEN FRENCH EXPLORERS ARRIVED IN INDIANA in the 1600s, the Shawnee, Potawatomie, Delaware, and Miami tribes already occupied the region, so it's no surprise that the name means "land of the Indians." As a result of the French and Indian War, the area was under British rule, but it passed to American hands after the Revolutionary War. In 1800 the Indiana Territory, which included much of the upper Midwest, was created. Under the leadership of Tecumseh, the Shawnee and other tribes struggled to retain their land. In 1811 the Native Americans were defeated in the deadly Battle of Tippecanoe. With plenty of land now available for farmers, Indiana's population grew large enough to be admitted as the 19th state on December 11, 1816.

—Mary Voors, Allen County Public Library

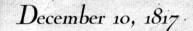

December 10, 1817

Mississippi

BY THE TIME MISSISSIPPI BECAME A U.S. TERRITORY IN 1798, the flags of France, Spain, and Britain had flown over its land. Following the Louisiana Purchase, cheap, fertile land became available, and cotton prices rose, creating a land boom. Many settlers came from the eastern part of the United States and northern Europe. These new settlers were happy to live in a territory of the U.S., but many immediately began working to gain statehood. In 1817 Congress divided the territory. The western part joined the Union as the state of Mississippi; the remaining land became the Alabama Territory. Mississippi held a convention to write a constitution, and statehood was granted later that year.

—Elizabeth Haynes, U. of Southern Mississippi

☆ Jackson

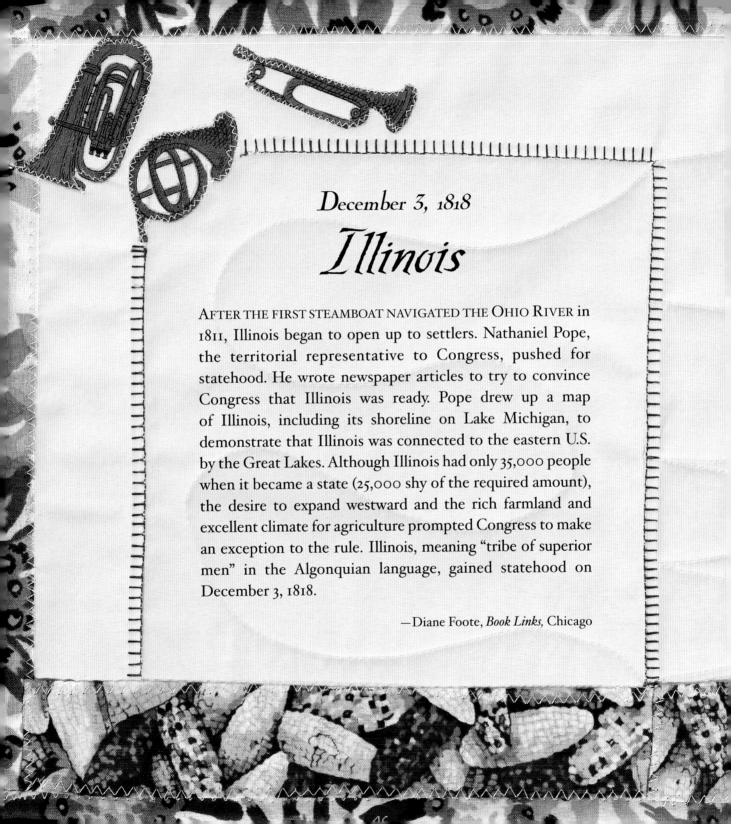

December 3, 1818

Illinois

AFTER THE FIRST STEAMBOAT NAVIGATED THE OHIO RIVER in 1811, Illinois began to open up to settlers. Nathaniel Pope, the territorial representative to Congress, pushed for statehood. He wrote newspaper articles to try to convince Congress that Illinois was ready. Pope drew up a map of Illinois, including its shoreline on Lake Michigan, to demonstrate that Illinois was connected to the eastern U.S. by the Great Lakes. Although Illinois had only 35,000 people when it became a state (25,000 shy of the required amount), the desire to expand westward and the rich farmland and excellent climate for agriculture prompted Congress to make an exception to the rule. Illinois, meaning "tribe of superior men" in the Algonquian language, gained statehood on December 3, 1818.

—Diane Foote, *Book Links,* Chicago

CHICAGO

★ Springfield

Montgomery

December 14, 1819

Alabama

IN 1763 THE FRENCH AND INDIAN WAR CAME TO AN END with the Treaty of Paris. The defeated French gave up control of almost all of their land on the continent of North America. The lands west of the Mississippi River went to Spain and lands east of the Mississippi went to Britain. Following the Revolutionary War, the region that is now Alabama was included in the Mississippi Territory, but the people of Alabama thought the territory was too big. As a result, Congress divided the territory in 1817. Alabama's fertile soil and forests lured settlers, and the population grew rapidly. A constitution was written in 1819, and Alabama proudly became the 22nd state.

—Tami Genry, Oak Mountain High School

The Missouri Compromise, 1820

By the time Missouri requested statehood in 1818, the bitter debate over slavery was beginning to divide the country. The invention of the cotton gin created a boom in the cotton industry, and the need for field workers ensured the use of slavery. One of the key compromises in the drafting of the Constitution had provided for slavery to continue in states that allowed it, forbidding consideration of the issue again until 1808.

In 1820 the Senate was evenly balanced between free and slave states. In an attempt to keep this balance, it was decided that when a slave state wanted to enter the Union, a nonslave state would also have to be admitted, and vice versa. This decision was known as the Missouri Compromise because at the time it was passed, Missouri was allowed to enter the Union as a slave state, while Maine was admitted as a free state. Congress divided the rest of the area, prohibiting slavery north of latitude 36 degrees 31 minutes — the Missouri Compromise line — while allowing slavery to exist south of that line.

Free states and territories

Slave states and territories

Unorganized Territory (closed to slavery in Missouri Comp.)

Arkansas Territory (open to slavery in Missouri Comp.)

Spanish possessions

Oregon Country (claimed by U.S. and Britain)

(part of) British Canada

Missouri Comp. line

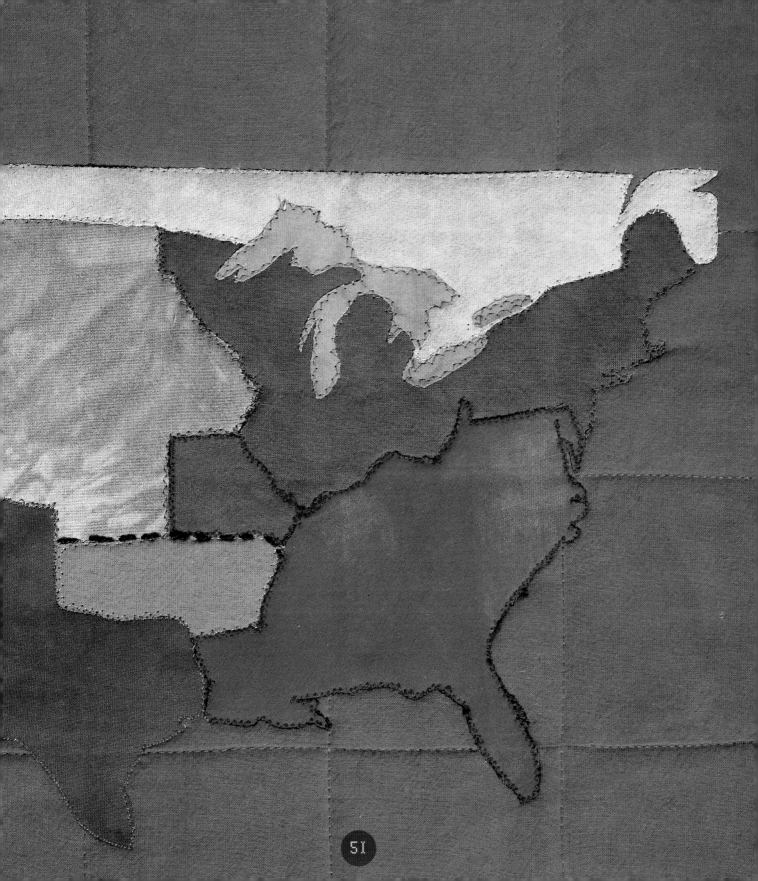

☆ Augusta

March 15, 1820

Maine

THE PEOPLE OF MAINE STARTED TO BECOME DISENCHANTED with their colonial overseers in 1691, when the British declared that all white pine trees of 24 inches in diameter belonged to Britain. This outraged Mainers because white pine trees were what they used to build masts for their thriving shipbuilding industry. Although Maine had been part of Massachusetts before it joined the United States, Mainers were a fiercely independent and determined people. They sought the right to have their own state. Their desire was fulfilled on March 15, 1820, when Maine officially became a state as part of the Missouri Compromise.

—Janet Lexow, Camden Public Library

August 10, 1821

Missouri

By 1819 Missouri territory had the required number of people, a constitution, and a clamoring citizenship wanting to join the Union. Missouri's request for statehood would not go unnoticed; instead it became the focus of a hot national debate. At the time, there were 11 free states and 11 slave states. Admitting Missouri to the Union would upset this balance, so Congress settled the problem with the Missouri Compromise. In exchange for allowing Missouri to be admitted as a slave state, Maine would be admitted as a free state. Congress also decided that except for Missouri, slavery would not be allowed in the lands of the Louisiana Purchase north of Missouri's southern border. Missouri joined the Union in 1821, making it the 24th state.

—Ann Sampson, North Central Missouri College

☆ Jefferson City

MISSOURI

ST. LOUIS

JOPLIN

June 15, 1836
Arkansas

ARKANSAS FIRST JOINED THE U.S. AS PART of the Louisiana Purchase. Then in 1819 it was established as a territory of its own. A rapid influx of white settlers entered the area during the 1830s following the U.S. government's relocation of Native Americans to Oklahoma reservations. In 1834 Ambrose H. Sevier, Arkansas's territorial delegate to Congress, realized that Michigan intended to petition for statehood as a free state. He knew it was Arkansas's chance to get into the Union—it would help to keep the balance of slave versus free states. With no way to communicate with the settlers back home, Sevier acted on his own, jumping at the opportunity to bring Arkansas into the Union as a slave state. The settlers accepted the wisdom of his actions and realized that without his quick thinking they could have been kept out of the Union for years. Arkansas became the 25th state in June of 1836.

—Bonnie M. Elliott, native Arkansan, U. of Texas, Austin

☆ Little Rock

☆ Lansing

January 26, 1837

Michigan

IN 1668 FATHER JACQUES MARQUETTE created the first permanent European settlement in Michigan, marking the beginning of French control of the area. The British gained the territory in 1763 following the French and Indian War. Twenty years later, the land passed to the newly formed United States. In 1787 Michigan became part of the Northwest Territory and, later, the Indiana Territory. In 1805 it finally became its own territory. At the time, many of Michigan's residents were former New Englanders eager for statehood. Though they wrote a state constitution in 1835, a dispute with Ohio over a strip of land near Toledo delayed Michigan's statehood. Eventually the two states agreed that Ohio would receive the Toledo Strip and Michigan would get the Upper Peninsula. Michigan became the 26th state on January 26, 1837.

—Vanessa Verdun-Morris, River Rouge Public Library

☆ Tallahassee

March 3, 1845
Florida

THE UNITED STATES RECEIVED THE LAND OF FLORIDA in
1819 as a payment for debts owed by the Spanish government. It was two more years before the U.S. officially
occupied Florida as a territory. As more settlers arrived,
pressure mounted to push out the native population who
had lived on the land for thousands of years. The Seminoles,
under the leadership of Osceola, resisted but eventually gave
in and moved west. Arguing that its admittance would bring
more people, wealth, and economic development to the
country, Florida was finally approved for statehood.
However, since it was a pro-slavery state, it had to be paired
for admittance with a non-slave-holding territory. In 1845
Iowa was ready too, and Florida became a state.

—Beverly Bass, LeRoy Collins Leon County Public Library

December 29, 1845

Texas

IN 1821 MEXICO AUTHORIZED STEPHEN F. AUSTIN to settle 300 families in its northern province of Texas. Soon, Mexico wasn't able to adequately govern Texas, and more settlers came than were authorized. Troubled by the illegal immigrants from the U.S., the Mexican government changed the rules for settlers, making life much more difficult for them. The Texans rebelled. In 1836 Texas declared its independence and months later won its freedom at San Jacinto. But the new Texas lacked resources to hold off attacks, settle land claims, and protect its borders. Many Texans wanted the stability of joining the U.S. The U.S. wanted the land, but feared that taking Texas would provoke war with Mexico. Finally, a resolution was adopted, and in 1845 Texas became a state. One provision gives the state the right to divide itself into four more states, but then Texas wouldn't have the bragging rights as the second largest state!

—Jeanette Larson, Austin Public Library

☆ Austin

☆ Des Moines

December 28, 1846

Iowa

ALTHOUGH WARNED THAT THERE MIGHT BE RIVER MONSTERS in it, Frenchmen Louis Joliet and Jacques Marquette traveled down the Iowa River in 1673 reaching the area now known as Iowa. Originally part of the Louisiana Purchase, Iowa became its own territory in 1838. The first governor, Robert Lucas, set up the new government. He wanted Iowa to become a state, but many were not as sure about the idea. If it remained a territory, the federal government would pay the salaries of its government officials. Once it was a state, Iowans would have to pay those salaries themselves through taxes. There were also disagreements over slavery and the state's boundaries. Finally, in 1844, Iowans were convinced that they had enough people to cover the expenses and would fare better economically as a state. On December 28, 1846, Iowa joined the United States.

— Shalar Brown, Iowa City Public Library

The Mexican War, 1848

The United States had feared that annexing Texas would spark a war with Mexico — and they were right. In 1846 on his last day in office, President John Tyler made Texas a state and set off a war. In 1848 the war ended with a U.S. victory and the Treaty of Guadalupe Hidalgo, in which the United States paid Mexico $15 million for all of Mexico's lands west of Texas, some 525,000 square miles. The war had not lasted long, but it changed our country forever.

The Mexican Cession greatly expanded our nation, as it contained the present-day states of California, Nevada, Utah, most of Arizona, and parts of New Mexico, Colorado, and Wyoming. In 1853 the U.S. acquired from Mexico the 29,640 square miles of the Gadsden Purchase for $10 million, completing the borders of the continental United States.

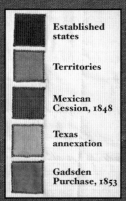

Established states

Territories

Mexican Cession, 1848

Texas annexation

Gadsden Purchase, 1853

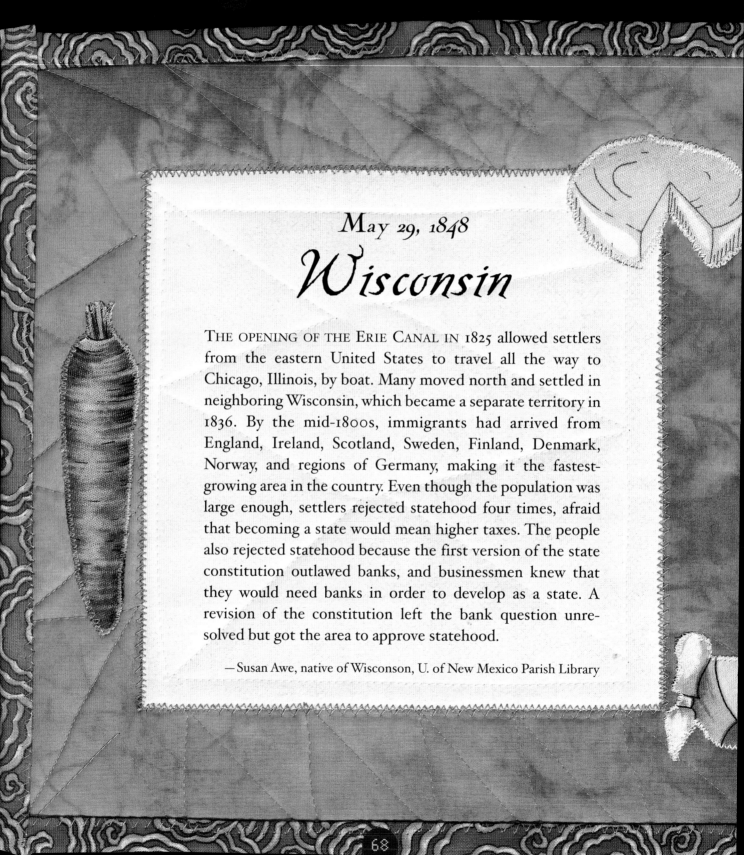

May 29, 1848

Wisconsin

THE OPENING OF THE ERIE CANAL IN 1825 allowed settlers from the eastern United States to travel all the way to Chicago, Illinois, by boat. Many moved north and settled in neighboring Wisconsin, which became a separate territory in 1836. By the mid-1800s, immigrants had arrived from England, Ireland, Scotland, Sweden, Finland, Denmark, Norway, and regions of Germany, making it the fastest-growing area in the country. Even though the population was large enough, settlers rejected statehood four times, afraid that becoming a state would mean higher taxes. The people also rejected statehood because the first version of the state constitution outlawed banks, and businessmen knew that they would need banks in order to develop as a state. A revision of the constitution left the bank question unresolved but got the area to approve statehood.

— Susan Awe, native of Wisconson, U. of New Mexico Parish Library

☆ Madison

September 9, 1850

California

CALIFORNIA WAS THE NAME OF A MYTHICAL ISLAND described in a 16th-century romance novel. In 1542 Juan Cabrillo, a Spanish explorer, claimed land along the Pacific coast of North America for Spain, naming it California after that fictional place. From that time on, California was governed at different times by Spain, Mexico, and finally the U.S. beginning in 1848. On January 24 of that same year, gold was discovered near Sacramento, and thousands of Americans came west to seek their fortunes, giving the state its nickname, "Golden State." The gold also drew the attention of the U.S. government. The non–Native American population had grown from 7,000 to 300,000 in less than three years. In 1849 48 delegates met to form a legislature, write a constitution, and declare themselves a state. On September 9, 1850, Congress made California the 31st state.

— Bessie Condos Tichauer, California State Library

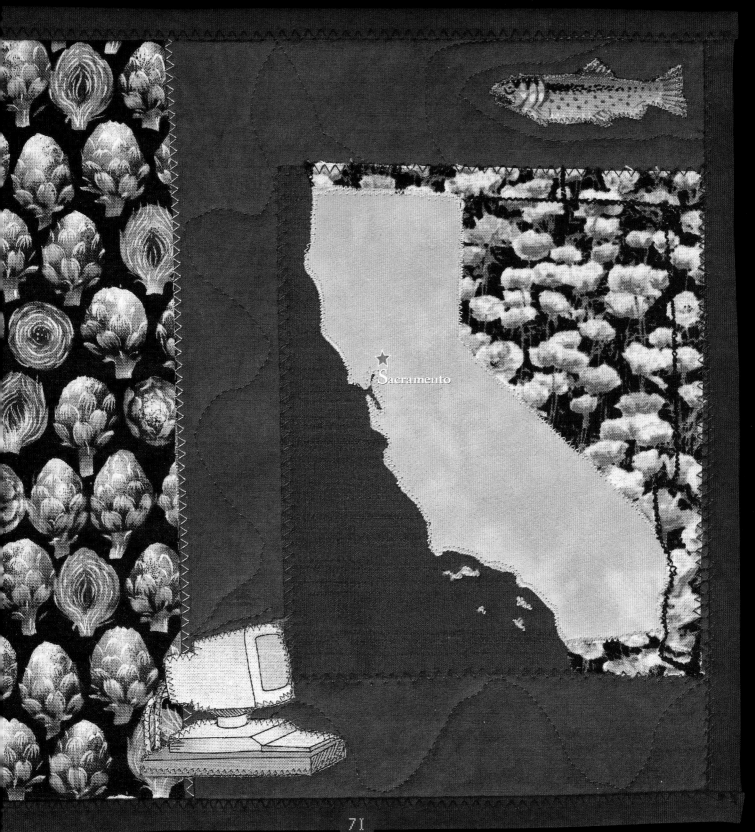

Sacramento

St. Paul

BEST BRAND SUGAR CORN

RYE

May 11, 1858

Minnesota

IN THE EARLY 1800S, SETTLERS GAVE MINNESOTA the nickname "Land of 10,000 Lakes," hoping to attract more people to the area. Since farmland in Europe was almost totally owned by hereditary landlords who'd had the land handed down from past generations, there was not much left for the average person. As a result, many Scandinavian, German, and Irish people were drawn to the fertile land of Minnesota. They came in droves, and by 1858 there were 150,000 people in the area, more than enough to qualify for statehood. The settlers pushed for statehood because they wanted tax–supported services such as roads, postal service, and public schools. In 1858 Minnesota became the 32nd state and qualified for these supports.

—Wendy Woodfill, Hennepin County Library

February 14, 1859

Oregon

IN 1804 PRESIDENT THOMAS JEFFERSON sent the explorers Lewis and Clark and their team to explore the region known as Oregon Country and to search for a Northwest Passage—a water route through the continent. They found no passage, but instead laid claim to the territory. For decades, Britain and the U.S. bickered over control of the area. After coming close to war, in 1848 the two countries settled their fight. The Treaty of Oregon was signed, and the Oregon Territory went to the U.S. For ten years, the issue of Oregon statehood was debated and dismissed. Despite large numbers of new settlers, some felt the population was too small and not ready for statehood. But the population and economy grew rapidly. Oregonians finally decided they wanted more control over their own government and agreed to statehood in 1859.

—Chris Weber, Atkinson Elementary School

☆ Salem

SWEET PEAS

Topeka

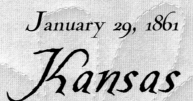

January 29, 1861

Kansas

THE KANSAS-NEBRASKA ACT OF 1854 cancelled part of the Missouri Compromise and gave each territory the right to decide about slavery within its own borders. When the Kansas territory was opened for settlement, residents from northern and southern states came into the area. The growing populations competed to see which could become a majority and then decide the slavery question. Violence erupted between the rival groups in what became known as "Bleeding Kansas." The anti-slavery side prevailed, and in 1859 a constitution for Kansas was submitted to Congress. Just before the outbreak of the Civil War, President Buchanan signed the bill, and Kansas entered the Union as a free state.

—Judy Druse, Mabee Library, Washburn U.

Secession, 1861

In 1860 Abraham Lincoln won the electoral votes of the free states (except New Jersey), ensuring him a victory in the election. Lincoln got less than 40 percent of the popular vote — almost none in the southern states. Before the election, many southern leaders, fearing he would put an end to slavery, threatened to leave the Union if Lincoln won. In December 1860 before Lincoln took office, South Carolina became the first state to leave the Union, followed by five other states: Mississippi, Florida, Alabama, Georgia, and Louisiana. Together, they formed the Confederate States of America. Within a few months, they were joined by Texas, Virginia, Arkansas, North Carolina, and Tennessee. The nation was torn, and a war had begun.

The Civil War (1861–1865) took more American lives than any other war in our history, before or since. Eleven states fought for the Confederacy and 23 states fought for the Union. In the end, the North won the war, and the country was reunited, but not happily.

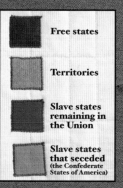

Free states

Territories

Slave states remaining in the Union

Slave states that seceded (the Confederate States of America)

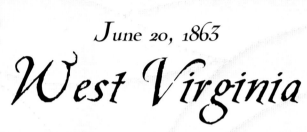

June 20, 1863
West Virginia

ORIGINALLY A PART OF VIRGINIA, WEST VIRGINIA was a new frontier, and its inhabitants, "Mountaineers," were very different from the wealthy plantation owners and enslaved farm workers in the rest of the state. Virginia's legislature voted to withdraw from the U.S. in 1861, but the people of western Virginia remained loyal to their country. They were opposed to seceding and felt unrepresented in Virginia. The U.S. Constitution says that no state can be divided without the consent of its legislative body, but President Lincoln proclaimed West Virginia a state of its own because the Union needed its natural resources, and Lincoln needed the votes in the next election. West Virginia is the only state created by a proclamation of the President and is the only state taken from another state without permission.

— Sandra Myers Wiseman, Ritchie and Woodsdale Elem. Schools

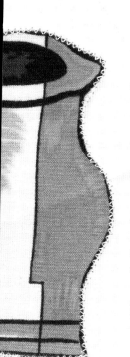

☆ Charleston

☆ Carson City

October 31, 1864
Nevada

A DECADE AFTER THE CALIFORNIA GOLD RUSH, miners struck gold near Virginia City. This discovery in 1859, known as the Comstock Lode, drew thousands to the area. Gold miners found a sticky blue-gray mud that clung to their shovels and picks and unwittingly discovered silver, too. Gold seekers headed east from California searching for wealth in the silver and gold ore of Nevada. People headed west to escape the financial troubles of the East Coast. By 1861 Nevada had become a separate territory. President Abraham Lincoln wanted Nevada to become a state for two reasons—most residents favored the Union and opposed slavery, and Nevada's silver could help pay for war expenses. Although Nevada did not have a sufficient population for statehood, the U.S. made an exception. Entering the Union during the Civil War, Nevada became known as the "Battle Born State."

— Cyndi Giorgis, U. of Nevada–Las Vegas

March 1, 1867

Nebraska

IN 1834 NEBRASKA WAS SET ASIDE BY THE U.S. as "Indian Territory," separate from any state or organized territory. The Ponca, Pawnee, and Santee Sioux then populated the area. In 1854, with the signing of the Kansas-Nebraska Act, the U.S. government broke its promise to the Native Americans and carved seven states out of the land promised to them. The act also declared that each state would have to decide if it wanted slavery. Nebraska's statehood was delayed as the two sides of the slavery debate continued to fight for their beliefs. As more and more settlers began to populate the rugged terrain, Nebraskans finally had to make this difficult decision. Even before Nebraska was officially admitted to the union in March of 1867 as the 37th state, slavery was outlawed there, providing strength to the Union as it faced the Civil War.

—Jennifer Miskec, Children's Literature Instructor, Omaha

☆ Lincoln

☆ Denver

August 1, 1876
Colorado

MOST OF THE AREA THAT WAS TO BECOME COLORADO joined the U.S. as part of the Louisiana Purchase. The rest came as part of the Treaty of Guadalupe Hidalgo with Mexico. The gold rush of 1859 brought thousands of miners and settlers to the area. Then, in 1862, the Homestead Act transformed the area. The new law gave large amounts of public land to the citizens. Any person who was the head of a household and was 21 years or older could receive 160 acres of land for a 10-dollar fee. Thousands of homesteaders flocked to the area to take up the offer, and development took off. Settlers hoped that the increased population would help Colorado to become a state, but the U.S. was busy fighting the Civil War. On August 1, 1876, during the celebration of 100 years of American independence, Colorado was finally admitted to the Union as the 38th state.

—Patricia Froehlich, Colorado State Library

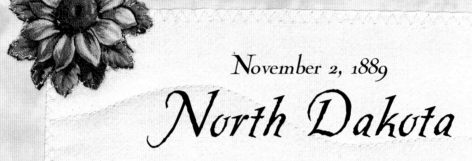

November 2, 1889

North Dakota

SETTLERS STARTED TO ARRIVE IN THE DAKOTA REGION after the Louisiana Purchase transferred the area from France to the U.S. In 1861 Congress created the Dakota Territory, which included all of present-day North Dakota and South Dakota and much of Wyoming and Montana. By 1886 over 100,000 people had settled the area. The people in the southern part of the territory did not like the appointed governor and decided they wanted to be a separate state of their own. They asked Congress to divide the territory into two states. Wanting to be fair, President Benjamin Harrison signed the bills to make the Dakota Territory into two states but kept secret which one was admitted as the 39th state and which as the 40th.

— Mary Reinertson-Sand, U. of North Dakota Center for Rural Health

☆ Bismarck

November 2, 1889
South Dakota

ALTHOUGH FUR TRADER LOUIS-JOSEPH AND EXPLORER François Vérendrye first visited the area that is now South Dakota in 1743, it was more than 100 years before farmers from Minnesota and Iowa began to settle the vast area. Congress created the Dakota Territory in 1861. When Gen. George A. Custer and his soldiers discovered gold in the Black Hills, people flooded into the territory. Much of the gold was on Lakota land, and the Lakota struggled to save their homeland and their culture but eventually were forced off their land. Settlers from the northern and southern parts of the territory could not agree on many things, so they asked Congress to divide the territory into two states. South Dakota joined the Union on November 2, 1889.

—LaVera Rose, South Dakota State Library

Pierre

Pheasant

☆ Helena

November 8, 1889
Montana

AFTER THE DISCOVERY OF GOLD THERE IN 1864, Montanans immediately began petitioning for admission to the Union so they could have the full constitutional rights enjoyed by other Americans. In 1866 Thomas Meagher, a Democratic territorial secretary, called a territorial convention to produce a written constitution. Apparently, on the way to the printer in St. Louis, Missouri, the constitution they had written disappeared. Meagher died mysteriously later that year. Over the next 20 years, Montanans applied for, but were denied, statehood because their constitution did not win congressional approval. It was not until 1889 that Congress passed an act permitting the territory to write another constitution and reapply for statehood. It was finally granted by President Benjamin Harrison in 1889.

—Don Spritzer, Missoula Public Library

November 11, 1889

Washington

FOLLOWING THE VOYAGE OF LEWIS AND CLARK, settlement in the Northwestern part of the country began to grow. In 1853 a group of citizens persuaded the government to split off the area north of the Columbia River, creating the Washington Territory. Recognizing the economic potential of the area's lumber, fishing, and mining industries, people flocked to Washington. In 1878 a constitution was written and submitted for approval. Railroads stretched to the territory and brought more settlers in the 1880s. Between 1880 and 1890, the state's population quadrupled. Eleven years after its constitution was submitted, Washington became the 42nd state.

—Viki Ash-Geisler, Spokane Public Library

☆ Olympia

July 3, 1890

Idaho

THE DISCOVERY OF GOLD IN IDAHO IN 1860 created a large population surge. A rich silver-mining industry attracted even more settlers to northern Idaho. As a result, Idaho gained enough people to form a state. Although the Native Americans who had lived on the land for thousands of years violently resisted efforts for statehood, all were defeated by 1877. Idaho became a state on July 3, 1890. Originally, President Benjamin Harrison was to sign the bill on July 4, but an Idaho representative learned that a state star was added to the national flag on the first Independence Day after a territory became a state, so the signing was changed to a day earlier. Although he claimed "Idaho" meant "gem of the mountain" in an Indian language, George M. Willing actually invented the name and had tried to convince Colorado to take it as its name.

—Jennifer Dunaway, Clearwater Memorial Public Library

☆ Boise

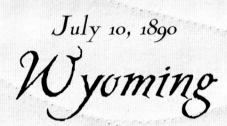

July 10, 1890
Wyoming

IN 1869, IN AN EFFORT TO INCREASE THE AREA'S POPULATION, the Wyoming territorial legislature granted unrestricted voting rights to women. Although this did help to spark population growth, Wyoming's liberal ideas actually worked against it. Some Congressmen did not want Wyoming's decision to grant women the right to vote to create a "bad" example for the rest of the country, and the territory's initial attempts at statehood were denied. Finally, in 1890, it became the 44th state, with voting rights for women remaining in its constitution. Wyoming's continued support of women's rights shone through in 1925 when the people of the state elected the first female governor in the United States.

—Jill Rourke, Wyoming State Library

Cheyenne
☆

Salt Lake City

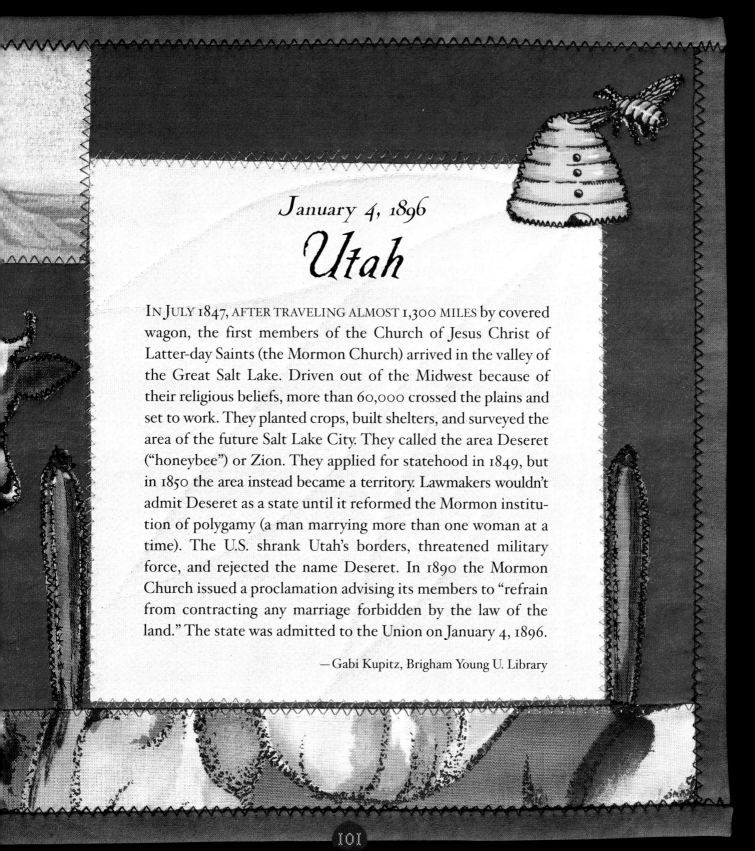

January 4, 1896
Utah

IN JULY 1847, AFTER TRAVELING ALMOST 1,300 MILES by covered wagon, the first members of the Church of Jesus Christ of Latter-day Saints (the Mormon Church) arrived in the valley of the Great Salt Lake. Driven out of the Midwest because of their religious beliefs, more than 60,000 crossed the plains and set to work. They planted crops, built shelters, and surveyed the area of the future Salt Lake City. They called the area Deseret ("honeybee") or Zion. They applied for statehood in 1849, but in 1850 the area instead became a territory. Lawmakers wouldn't admit Deseret as a state until it reformed the Mormon institution of polygamy (a man marrying more than one woman at a time). The U.S. shrank Utah's borders, threatened military force, and rejected the name Deseret. In 1890 the Mormon Church issued a proclamation advising its members to "refrain from contracting any marriage forbidden by the law of the land." The state was admitted to the Union on January 4, 1896.

— Gabi Kupitz, Brigham Young U. Library

☆Oklahoma City

November 16, 1907
Oklahoma

IN THE EARLY 1820S SOME STATES, such as Georgia and Alabama, began rumbling about wanting to have their Indians relocated to other areas. Although Plains Indians had lived in the Oklahoma region for centuries, tribes of the southeast were forced by the government to move there, too. The area was defined as "Indian Territory." Following the Civil War, a booming cattle industry brought cowboys to Oklahoma. When the U.S. opened the territory to white settlers in 1889, thousands rushed in to claim land and ended up discovering oil in the area. Many territory leaders wanted statehood so that locally elected officials could control land rich in natural resources. Native Americans wanted an independent Indian state to provide a haven for their people. In 1907 the Indian and Oklahoma territories united, and a symbolic wedding between a cowboy and an Indian maiden marked the entrance of Oklahoma to the Union.

—Twyla Camp, U. of Oklahoma

January 6, 1912

New Mexico

IN 1821 MEXICO, WHICH THEN INCLUDED THE AREA now called New Mexico, gained independence from Spain. Americans began entering the area to settle, and in 1846, during the Mexican War, the U.S. seized the territory. The 1848 Treaty of Guadalupe Hidalgo ended the war and led the way for the establishment of the territory of New Mexico in 1850. New Mexicans were eager to join the U.S., but were opposed by many other Americans who felt that the population was too different from the rest of the country. They were thought of as "too Catholic" and "too foreign." There was also conflict between the Hispanic New Mexicans and the "Anglo" New Mexicans, many of whom originated from southern states. New Mexico's service to the Union during the Civil War, and later in the Spanish American War, helped change attitudes. After drawing up a constitution in 1911, New Mexico achieved statehood in 1912.

—Gayle Travis, Lomas Tramway Library

☆ Santa Fe

NEW MEXICO

February 14, 1912

Arizona

IN 1848, AS A RESULT OF THE GUADALUPE HIDALGO TREATY, northern Arizona became part of the United States. The rest of Arizona became a U.S. territory through the Gadsden Purchase in 1853. Although Arizona wanted to become a state in 1910, President Taft vetoed the bill because he did not like parts of the territory's constitution. Arizona's constitution, written during the "Progressive era," contained reform provisions including workers' compensation, short terms for elected officials, voting rights for women, and the barring of trusts and monopolies from the state. Congress was also fearful that Arizona would send Democrats to Congress, which might shift the balance of power. After certain clauses were removed, Arizona became the last of the lower 48 states to enter the Union.

—Tim Wadham, Maricopa County Library District

☆ Phoenix

The Lower 48, 1912-1959

At the end of the War Between the States, all the parts of what would become the lower 48 states were assembled. But much territory remained unsettled and undeveloped. As had often been the case in the past, states were admitted to the Union when they reached a certain level of population, development, and political organization. Those seeking admission for their state often saw statehood as a vehicle for greater economic and population growth. When Arizona was admitted as the 48th state in 1912, the quilt of states of the contiguous United States was completed. Within five years of Arizona's statehood, the U.S. entered World War I. Our country banded together and fought with American pride.

It was several decades until another state would join our Union. Americans experienced many struggles and successes in that time including World War I, the Depression, Prohibition, and World War II. Through all of its experiences, our country held together. It was a land that stretched from sea to shining sea, measuring from east to west approximately 3,000 miles.

January 3, 1959
Alaska

IN 1867 U.S. SECRETARY OF STATE WILLIAM SEWARD negotiated the purchase of Alaska from Russia for 7.2 million dollars. Many Americans thought it was a huge mistake to buy land covered by 100,000 glaciers, and they nicknamed Alaska "Seward's Folly." The gold rush of 1897 proved them all wrong. At a cost of less than two cents an acre, America had gotten a great deal! Between 1890 and 1900, Alaska's population doubled, and it became a territory in 1912. After World War I, adventurous pilots settled in Alaska, where they could transport people, mail, and goods around the territory. After World War II, another population explosion occurred when the U.S. military expanded into the state. In the 1950s Alaskans sought statehood as a means of controlling development and the exploitation of their rich resources by outsiders. In 1959, 47 years after Arizona, Alaska became the 49th state.

—Ann K. Symons, Juneau Douglas High School Library

Juneau ☆

Honolulu

August 21, 1959
Hawaii

POLYNESIANS IN OUTRIGGER CANOES CAME TO HAWAII about 1,500 years ago. By 1810 the Hawaiian Islands were united, ruled by King Kamehameha the Great, but life in Hawaii changed dramatically with the continued arrival of foreigners. Hawaii's location in the middle of the Pacific Ocean, its rich crops, and its importance as a supply port made it attractive to American business. In 1898 Hawaii was annexed and a territorial government was established two years later. Although many natives did not want to become part of the U.S., others longed for Hawaii to become a state. The resistance came partly from American fear of the island people, as well as the fear that Hawaii was too far away from the mainland to become a part of the country. In 1947 the House of Representatives enacted legislation to approve Hawaii. After delays from the Korean War, statehood was finally granted to this island paradise in 1959.

—Dave Del Rocco, Hawaii State Library

HAWAIIAN
HAZELNUT
NET WT   8 OZ.

The United States of America

With the 1959 admission of Alaska and Hawaii to the Union, our quilt of states became complete — a nation spanning North America and stretching thousands of miles into the Pacific Ocean. The geographic location of the western states encourages our involvement with other nations bordering the Pacific Basin, just as the location of the original 13 Colonies on the Atlantic seaboard began our involvement with Europe. Could the citizens of the original 13 Colonies have imagined in the 1770s the vast nation of the United States in the 21st century? Our expansive geography and the global political, economic, and cultural influence that comes with it leave an important responsibility in the hands of each successive generation of citizens of our united quilt of states.

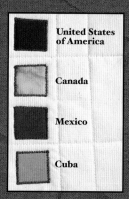

United States of America

Canada

Mexico

Cuba

State Facts

(States are listed in alphabetical order; their order of entrance into the Union is included)

Alabama   #22
Date of statehood: December 14, 1819
State slogan/nickname: Heart of Dixie
State tree: Longleaf pine
State flower: Camellia
State bird: Northern flicker
Fun fact: The name "Alabama" comes from the Choctaw language and means "thicket clearers."
A state claim to fame: Helen Keller was born in Tuscumbia, Alabama, in 1880.

Alaska   #49
Date of statehood: January 3, 1959
State slogan/nickname: Last Frontier
State tree: Sitka spruce
State flower: Forget-me-not
State bird: Willow ptarmigan
Fun fact: Alaska's flag—eight gold stars on a field of blue—was designed by Benny Benson, a child, in a flag contest.
A state claim to fame: Alaska is the only state with dog mushing as the state sport.

Arizona   #48
Date of statehood: February 14, 1912
State slogan/nickname: Grand Canyon State
State tree: Paloverde
State flower: Saguaro
State bird: Cactus wren
Fun fact: The saguaro cactus, which produces the state flower, may take 200 years to reach its full height of as much as 50 feet tall.
A state claim to fame: As represented by the color of the large star in the middle of its flag, Arizona produces the most copper of any state.

Arkansas   #25
Date of statehood: June 15, 1836
State slogan/nickname: Natural State
State tree: Pine
State flower: Apple blossom
State bird: Mockingbird
Fun fact: In 1962, Sam Walton opened a small store in Rogers, Arkansas. Wal-Mart is now the largest retail corporation in the world.
A state claim to fame: The New Madrid earthquake, the most powerful ever to hit the lower 48 states, struck northeast Arkansas in 1811. It is ranked as one of the 20 greatest earthquakes to occur anywhere in the world.

California   #31
Date of statehood: September 9, 1850
State slogan/nickname: Golden State
State tree: California redwood
State flower: Golden poppy
State bird: California valley quail
Fun fact: California has the largest population of any state, and one of every eight people in the U.S. lives in California.
A state claim to fame: California has the world's tallest tree, a coast redwood, that stands 368 feet tall.

Colorado   #38
Date of statehood: August 1, 1876
State slogan/nickname: Centennial State
State tree: Colorado blue spruce
State flower: Columbine
State bird: Lark bunting
Fun fact: The 13th step of the state capitol building in Denver is exactly one mile above sea level, giving the city the nickname "Mile High City," although it is not the highest city in the U.S.
A state claim to fame: Colorado became the 38th state during the U.S. Centennial year.

Connecticut   #5
Date of statehood: January 9, 1788
State slogan/nickname: Constitution State
State tree: White oak
State flower: Mountain laurel
State bird: Robin
Fun fact: The name Connecticut comes from the Native American word "Quinatucquet," which means "Beside the Long Tidal River."
A state claim to fame: The nation's oldest daily newspaper in continuous existence, *The Hartford Courant*, was founded in 1764.

Delaware   #1
Date of statehood: December 7, 1787
State slogan/nickname: First State
State tree: American holly
State flower: Peach blossom
State bird: Blue hen chicken
Fun fact: Legends say that Blackbeard, Captain Kidd, and other pirates buried their treasure in different spots within Delaware.
A state claim to fame: Rehobeth Beach in southern Delaware attracts so many tourists from Washington, D.C., that it is known as the Nation's Summer Capital.

Florida   #27
Date of statehood: March 3, 1845
State slogan/nickname: Sunshine State
State tree: Sabal palmetto palm
State flower: Orange blossom
State bird: Mockingbird
Fun fact: Florida has a designated state marine mammal. It is the manatee.
A state claim to fame: The alligator is the state reptile, and more than one millio[n] alligators live in Florida.

Georgia   #4
Date of statehood: January 2, 1788
State slogan/nickname: Empire State o[f] the South
State tree: Live oak
State flower: Cherokee rose
State bird: Brown thrasher
Fun fact: Coca-Cola, made of 99 percent water and sugar, along with cinnamon, van[illa,] lime juice, and a mystery ingredient, was invented in Atlanta, the state capital.
A state claim to fame: In 1912 Juliette Gordon Lowe founded the Girl Scouts in Savannah.

Hawaii   #50
Date of statehood: August 21, 1959
State slogan/nickname: Aloha State
State tree: Kukul (Candlenut)
State flower: Yellow hibiscus
State bird: Hawaiian goose (Nene)
Fun fact: Aloha is a Hawaiian greeting th[at] means hello, goodbye, love, and other thin[gs.]
A state claim to fame: Hawaii is the onl[y] state made up of islands. There are eight m[ain] islands, and the chain of islands extends al[most] 1,600 miles. Hawaii is the most isolated gr[oup] of islands in the world. It is over 2,500 mil[es] from North America.

Idaho   #43
Date of statehood: July 3, 1890
State slogan/nickname: Gem State
State tree: White pine
State flower: Syringa (Mock orange)
State bird: Mountain bluebird
Fun fact: Shelley, Idaho, is the home of th[e] Idaho Annual Spud Day.
A state claim to fame: Hell's Canyon is t[he] deepest gorge in the United States, measur[ing] 7,993 feet deep and ten miles from rim to r[im.]

nois   #21
te of statehood: December 3, 1818
te slogan/nickname: Land of Lincoln
te tree: White oak
te flower: Violet
te bird: Cardinal
n fact: Ray Kroc opened the first
Donald's restaurant in Des Plaines, Illinois,
955. A re-creation of that first restaurant
ow a museum.
state claim to fame: Abraham Lincoln,
became the 16th President of the United
tes in 1861, lived most of his life in Illinois.

iana   #19
te of statehood: December 11, 1816
te slogan/nickname: Hoosier State
te tree: Tulip poplar
te flower: Peony
te bird: Cardinal
n fact: People who live in Indiana are called
osiers, but although it is one of the oldest
knames, nobody knows where the word
e from.
state claim to fame: More major highways
ersect in Indiana than in any other state,
king Indiana the "Crossroads of America."

va   #29
te of statehood: December 28, 1846
te slogan/nickname: Hawkeye State
te tree: Oak
te flower: Wild rose
te bird: Eastern goldfinch
n fact: Amelia Jenks Bloomer, an Iowa
ive, worked hard for women's rights.
started a trend of women wearing comfort-
e, loose-fitting pants, named "bloomers"
er honor.
state claim to fame: With the Missouri
the west and the Mississippi on the east,
va is the only state to be bordered by two
jor navigable rivers.

nsas   #34
te of statehood: January 29, 1861
te slogan/nickname: Sunflower State
te tree: Cottonwood
te flower: Sunflower
te bird: Western meadowlark
n fact: Kansas citizens are called Jayhawks.
gend says a pioneer once started across
nsas with a bare minimum of provisions,
ing he would complete his journey by "jay-
wking" his way.
state claim to fame: The geographic
ter of the continental United States is
ated in north central Kansas.

Kentucky   #15
Date of statehood: June 1, 1792
State slogan/nickname: Bluegrass State
State tree: Tulip poplar
State flower: Goldenrod
State bird: Cardinal
Fun fact: On nights of a full moon, a "moon-
bow," appears at Cumberland Falls. This hap-
pens when the moon shines through the mist.
A state claim to fame: Mammoth Cave is
the world's longest cave system.

Louisiana   #18
Date of statehood: April 30, 1812
State slogan/nickname: Pelican State
State tree: Cypress
State flower: Magnolia
State bird: Eastern brown pelican
Fun fact: Known for its celebration of Mardi
Gras, Louisiana held its first organized parade
in New Orleans in 1838.
A state claim to fame: Louisiana is the birth-
place of jazz music.

Maine   #23
Date of statehood: March 15, 1820
State slogan/nickname: Pine Tree State
State tree: Eastern white pine
State flower: White pine cone and tassel
State bird: Chickadee
Fun fact: The moose is the state animal, and
the Maine coon, one of the oldest American
cat breeds, is the state cat.
A state claim to fame: It's the only state in
the nation with only one syllable in its name.

Maryland   #7
Date of statehood: April 28, 1788
State slogan/nickname: Old Line State
State tree: White oak
State flower: Black-eyed Susan
State bird: Northern (Baltimore) oriole
Fun fact: In 2003 the thoroughbred was
declared the state horse.
A state claim to fame: It's the only state that
has jousting, a sport that retains the pageantry
of medieval times, as its state sport.

Massachusetts   #6
Date of statehood: February 6, 1788
State slogan/nickname: Bay State
State tree: American elm
State flower: Mayflower
State bird: Chickadee
Fun fact: Boston cream pie is the state dessert.
A state claim to fame: The state cookie,
chocolate chip, was invented in 1930 at the
Toll House Restaurant.

Michigan   #26
Date of statehood: January 26, 1837
State slogan/nickname: Great Lake State
State tree: White pine
State flower: Apple blossom
State bird: Robin
Fun fact: The shores of Michigan hold more
than 115 lighthouses.
A state claim to fame: Michigan borders
four of the five Great Lakes.

Minnesota   #32
Date of statehood: May 11, 1858
State slogan/nickname: Gopher State
State tree: Red pine
State flower: Showy lady's slipper
State bird: Common loon
Fun fact: Part of Minnesota is farther north
than any other state in the lower 48.
A state claim to fame: In 1922 water skiing
was invented at Lake Pepin, Minnesota.

Mississippi   #20
Date of statehood: December 10, 1817
State slogan/nickname: Magnolia State
State tree: Magnolia
State flower: Magnolia
State bird: Mockingbird
Fun fact: In 1902 President Theodore
Roosevelt refused to shoot a bear cub while
hunting in Mississippi. This led to the creation
of a stuffed toy called Teddy's Bear.
A state claim to fame: The longest man-made
beach in the world, from Biloxi to Henderson Point.

Missouri   #24
Date of statehood: August 10, 1821
State slogan/nickname: Show Me State
State tree: Dogwood
State flower: Hawthorn
State bird: Eastern bluebird
Fun fact: Attendees ate two new foods at
the St. Louis World's Fair (the first in the U.S.)
in 1904—hot dogs and ice-cream cones.
A state claim to fame: Kansas City is second
only to Rome, Italy, as the city with the most
fountains in the world.

Montana   #41
Date of statehood: November 8, 1889
State slogan/nickname: Treasure State
State tree: Ponderosa pine
State flower: Bitterroot
State bird: Western meadowlark
Fun fact: The state animal is the grizzly bear.
A state claim to fame: Jeannette Rankin,
the first woman to serve in the U.S. Congress,
represented Montana.

Nebraska #37

Date of statehood: March 1, 1867
State slogan/nickname: Cornhusker State
State tree: Cottonwood
State flower: Goldenrod
State bird: Western meadowlark
Fun fact: In 1927 Edwin Perkins developed Kool-Aid in Hastings, Nebraska. Kool-Aid is now the state soft drink.
A state claim to fame: Large portions of the state are covered by sand, making central Nebraska the largest area of sand dunes in North America.

Nevada #36

Date of statehood: October 31, 1864
State slogan/nickname: Silver State
State tree: Single-leaf piñon and bristlecone pine
State flower: Sagebrush
State bird: Mountain bluebird
Fun fact: Eighty-five percent of Nevada's land is federally owned, including Area 51, the secret air base that gives the area its title as "UFO Capital of the World."
A state claim to fame: Some of the largest fossils of ichthyosaurs, prehistoric reptiles measuring 50 feet long and 8 feet around, have been discovered in Berlin, Nevada.

New Hampshire #9

Date of statehood: June 21, 1788
State slogan/nickname: Granite State
State tree: White birch
State flower: Purple lilac
State bird: Purple finch
Fun fact: The ladybug has been the state insect since 1977, when fifth graders in Concord campaigned for its adoption.
A state claim to fame: A large natural piece of granite in the White Mountains that formed a profile of an old man—The Old Man of the Mountain—was the state symbol until its collapse on May 3, 2003.

New Jersey #3

Date of statehood: December 18, 1787
State slogan/nickname: Garden State
State tree: Red oak
State flower: Violet
State bird: Eastern goldfinch
Fun fact: The game Monopoly is based on streets in Atlantic City, where the first Miss America pageant was held in 1921 to encourage tourists to stay through Labor Day.
A state claim to fame: The first college football game in the world was played between two New Jersey colleges, Rutgers and Princeton, on November 6, 1869.

New Mexico #47

Date of statehood: January 6, 1912
State slogan/nickname: Land of Enchantment
State tree: Piñon
State flower: Yucca
State bird: Roadrunner
Fun fact: New Mexico even has a state question—"Red or green?" It means "How do you want your chile?"
A state claim to fame: Santa Fe is the oldest capital city in the U.S., founded in 1610.

New York #11

Date of statehood: July 26, 1788
State slogan/nickname: Empire State
State tree: Sugar maple
State flower: Rose
State bird: Eastern bluebird
Fun fact: Although New York City is the largest city in the country with more than eight million people, the majority of the state is still rural. More than 60 percent of the land is covered with forests.
A state claim to fame: Niagara Falls, where more than 150,000 gallons of water rush over the edge every second.

North Carolina #12

Date of statehood: November 21, 1789
State slogan/nickname: Tar Heel State
State tree: Pine
State flower: Dogwood
State bird: Cardinal
Fun fact: The Plott Hound, a fearless hunting dog with a bugle-like call, is the state dog.
A state claim to fame: Orville Wright flew the first power-driven airplane at Kill Devil Hills on December 17, 1903, staying in the air for 12 seconds on his first trip.

North Dakota #39

Date of statehood: November 2, 1889
State slogan/nickname: Flickertail State
State tree: American elm
State flower: Wild prairie rose
State bird: Western meadowlark
Fun fact: Square dancing is the state dance.
A state claim to fame: Farms cover 90 percent of North Dakota's land, making it the most rural state in the nation.

Ohio #17

Date of statehood: March 1, 1803
State slogan/nickname: Buckeye State
State tree: Buckeye
State flower: Scarlet carnation
State bird: Cardinal
Fun fact: Ohio is the only state that has a pennant-shaped flag.
A state claim to fame: One of the largest roller coaster parks in the world, with 16 roller coasters, is at Cedar Point in Sandusky.

Oklahoma #46

Date of statehood: November 16, 1907
State slogan/nickname: Sooner State
State tree: Redbud
State flower: Mistletoe
State bird: Scissor-tailed flycatcher
Fun fact: The Indian blanket, a colorful red-and-yellow flower, is the state wildflower.
A state claim to fame: Beaver, Oklahoma, holds the World Cow Chip Throwing Championship every April.

Oregon #33

Date of statehood: February 14, 1859
State slogan/nickname: Beaver State
State tree: Douglas fir
State flower: Oregon grape
State bird: Western meadowlark
Fun fact: Mount Hood, Oregon's highest mountain, is the second most climbed mountain in the world. (The most climbed is Mount Fuji in Japan.)
A state claim to fame: Oregon grows 99 percent of the country's hazelnuts, the state nut.

Pennsylvania #2

Date of statehood: December 12, 1787
State slogan/nickname: Keystone State
State tree: Hemlock
State flower: Mountain laurel
State bird: Ruffled grouse
Fun fact: The state got its nickname because there were six colonies north of it and six colonies south of it, when it was a colony.
A state claim to fame: Pennsylvania is the birthplace of the U.S. Constitution and the Declaration of Independence, giving it another nickname—"Birthstate of the Nation."

Rhode Island #13

Date of statehood: May 29, 1790
State slogan/nickname: Ocean State
State tree: Red maple
State flower: Violet
State bird: Rhode Island red (chicken)
Fun fact: The oldest indoor shopping mall in the U.S. is the Arcade, built in 1828 in Providence.
A state claim to fame: This smallest state in the nation has the longest official name: The State of Rhode Island and Providence Plantations.

uth Carolina #8
ate of statehood: May 23, 1788
ate slogan/nickname: Palmetto State
ate tree: Palmetto
ate flower: Yellow jessamine
ate bird: Carolina wren
n fact: The Boykin spaniel, developed
create a small retriever that would fit into
ats, is the state dog.
state claim to fame: The Shag, a type
swing dance developed in the 1940s by
nagers, is the state dance. "Shaggers"
her in Myrtle Beach every year for the
ional championships.

uth Dakota #40
ate of statehood: November 2, 1889
ate slogan/nickname: Mount Rushmore
ate
ate tree: Black Hills spruce
ate flower: Pasqueflower
ate bird: Chinese ring-necked pheasant
n fact: Kuchen, a German sweet treat
de with cream cheese and fruit, is the
te dessert.
state claim to fame: Sue the dinosaur,
largest, most complete, and best-preserved
annosaurus rex fossil found in North
nerica, was discovered on the Cheyenne
ver Indian Reservation.

nnessee #16
ate of statehood: June 1, 1796
ate slogan/nickname: Volunteer State
ate tree: Tulip poplar
ate flower: Iris
ate bird: Mockingbird
n fact: Tennessee has more than 3,800
res across the state.
state claim to fame: Both blues and
k-and-roll were born here. Music is so
egral to this state that Tennessee has
e official state songs.

xas #28
ate of statehood: December 29, 1845
ate slogan/nickname: Lone Star State
ate tree: Pecan
ate flower: Bluebonnet
ate bird: Mockingbird
n fact: Dr Pepper soda was created by a
ung pharmacist in Waco, Texas, in 1885. Once
led the "King of Beverages," Dr. Pepper is
e oldest major soft-drink brand in America.
state claim to fame: Texas is the "battiest"
te in the Union—three-quarters of bat
cies spend time in Texas.

Utah #45
Date of statehood: January 4, 1896
State slogan/nickname: Beehive State
State tree: Blue spruce
State flower: Sego lily
State bird: California gull
Fun fact: The Kennecott Bingham Canyon Copper Mine is the world's largest open-pit copper mine. It is so deep that two Sears Towers stacked on top of each other would not reach the top of the mine. Space-shuttle astronauts could see the mine from space as they passed over the United States.
A state claim to fame: The Great Salt Lake is the largest saltwater lake in North America.

Vermont #14
Date of statehood: March 4, 1791
State slogan/nickname: Green Mountain State
State tree: Sugar maple
State flower: Red clover
State bird: Hermit thrush
Fun fact: The first American Boy Scout troop was founded in Barre in 1909.
A state claim to fame: Vermont is the largest producer of maple syrup in the country.

Virginia #10
Date of statehood: June 25, 1788
State slogan/nickname: Old Dominion State
State tree: Dogwood
State flower: Flowering dogwood
State bird: Cardinal
Fun fact: Milk is the state beverage.
A state claim to fame: Virginia is often referred to as the "Mother of Presidents" because it is the birthplace of eight U.S. Presidents, including seven of the first twelve leaders.

Washington #42
Date of statehood: November 11, 1889
State slogan/nickname: Evergreen State
State tree: Western hemlock
State flower: Coast rhododendron
State bird: Willow goldfinch
Fun fact: The Olympic Peninsula, in western Washington, is home to one of the world's northernmost rain forests. Kenai rain forest in Alaska is the northernmost.
A state claim to fame: Washington is the only state named after a U.S. President.

West Virginia #35
Date of statehood: June 20, 1863
State slogan/nickname: Mountain State
State tree: Sugar maple

State flower: Rhododendron
State bird: Cardinal
Fun fact: The state is sometimes called "America's Little Switzerland" because it has the highest average altitude of any state east of the Mississippi.
A state claim to fame: At least nine rivers will give you a wild ride here, including the New River, which is one of the oldest rivers in North America. West Virginia is often called the Whitewater Capital of the East.

Wisconsin #30
Date of statehood: May 29, 1848
State slogan/nickname: Badger State
State tree: Sugar maple
State flower: Wood violet
State bird: Robin
Fun fact: In 1847 the U.S. Olympic Circus, the largest traveling circus in America at the time, made Delavan, Wisconsin, its winter home. The P.T. Barnum Circus ("The Greatest Show on Earth") was founded in Delavan in 1871, and the Ringling brothers came from Baraboo, Wisconsin. These help give the state its nickname as "The Mother of Circuses."
A state claim to fame: Green Bay's paper mills make it the Toilet Paper Capital of the World.

Wyoming #44
Date of statehood: July 10, 1890
State slogan/nickname: Equality State
State tree: Plains cottonwood
State flower: Indian paintbrush
State bird: Western meadowlark
Fun fact: Wyoming was home to more than 50 different types of dinosaurs. Wyoming's dinosaur skeletons are on display in museums all over the world.
A state claim to fame: Wyoming is home to Yellowstone, the first national park in the United States, and the mysterious Devil's Tower, the first national monument in the U.S.

Contributors

Alabama: Tami Genry is a media specialist at Oak Mountain H.S. She enjoys being with her husband, Tim, and children, Caleb, Colby, Laci, and Landon.

Alaska: Ann K. Symons is a school librarian. She has worked for the Juneau School District for 26 years and also served as president of ALA.

Arizona: Tim Wadham is a children's services coordinator in the Maricopa Cty. Library.

Arkansas: Bonnie M. Elliott is a lecturer at the U. of Texas at Austin. She shares her love of children's literature with preservice teachers.

California: Bessie Condos Tichauer, a youth services specialist at the state library, has served on ALA Council, Newbery, and Caldecott committees.

Colorado: Patricia Froehlich is a consultant at the state library who enjoys working with youth service librarians from every corner of her state.

Connecticut: Veronica Stevenson-Moudamane is Manager of Junior Services at Danbury Library. One of her goals is to visit all 50 states by age 50.

Delaware: Melissa Rabey is a librarian at the Brandywine Hundred Library. As a native, she is happy to see a book include her favorite state.

Florida: Beverly Bass is manager of the Fort Braden branch of LeRoy Collins Leon Cty. Public Library.

Georgia: Janis Hayden is a school library media specialist at Eagle's Landing M.S. in McDonough. She's been in education for more than 30 years.

Hawaii: David Del Rocco has been a librarian in the public library system in Hawaii for 14 years. He now works in the Hawaii and Pacific Section.

Idaho: Jennifer Dunaway is a children's programs librarian at Clearwater Memorial Public Library.

Illinois: Diane Foote is associate editor of *Book Links*. She lives in Chicago with her family.

Indiana: Mary Voors is a children's services manager with Allen Cty. Public Library.

Iowa: Shalar Brown has worked in children's services at public libraries for more than 15 years. Her sons, Spencer and Harrison, enjoy the many perks of being "library kids."

Kansas: Judy Druse works in a curriculum library at Washburn U. and helps future teachers.

Kentucky: James C. Klotter is the state historian and a professor at Georgetown College. He is the author, co-author, or editor of 16 books.

Louisiana: Patricia Austin, a published author, is a professor of children's literature at the U. of New Orleans.

Maine: Janet Lexow is a librarian at Camden Public Library in Camden, Maine.

Maryland: Stacy Brown works at Judith Resnik E.S. in Gaithersburg, Maryland.

Massachusetts: Mary Ann Tourjee is Youth services consultant for the Central Masssachusetts Regional Library System. She is an advocate for children and literacy.

Michigan: Vanessa Verdun-Morris is a youth services librarian in Dearborn Heights. She loves comic books and introducing kids to graphic novels.

Minnesota: Wendy Woodfill is the children's selection librarian for Hennepin Cty. On Saturdays she and her daughter like to snuggle up and read.

Mississippi: Elizabeth Haynes teaches at the School of Library and Info. Science at the U. of Southern Mississippi. This born-and-bred Texan is enjoying her sojourn in the Deep South.

Missouri: Ann Sampson is a librarian at North Central Missouri College in Trenton. She is active in information literacy instruction.

Montana: Don Spritzer is a reference librarian for Missoula Public Library.

Nebraska: Jennifer Miskec teaches children's literature to preservice elementary teachers.

Nevada: Cyndi Giorgis, an assoc. professor of literature education at U. of NV, has written widely, and served on Caldecott and Newbery committees.

New Hampshire: Ann Hoey is the Youth service coordinator at the State Library. She's also been a children's librarian and an English teacher.

New Jersey: Honi Wasserman is a media specialist at Wyoming E.S. in Millburn. She loves connecting books and kids.

New Mexico: Gayle Travis was born and raised in her state (she can't give up the mountains and green chile) and has been a librarian for 15 years.

New York: Starr LaTronica was born in the Bronx, grew up in Iowa, and became a librarian in California. She's been a youth services manager for the Four Cty. Library System for the past 10 years.

North Carolina: Pamela Barron is a professor in the UNC Dept. of Library and Info. Studies. Since 1966, she's worked with kids in libraries.

North Dakota: Mary Reinertson-Sand is a librarian at the UND Center for Rural Healt She's worked in libraries for over 20 years.

Ohio: Sue McCleaf Nespeca is an early litera and children's literature consultant and head Kid Lit Plus Consulting in Youngstown.

Oklahoma: Twyla Camp is a graduate assist at the U. of OK School of Library and Info. St

Oregon: Chris Weber is a teacher at Atkins E.S. in Portland. He loves teaching, writing, trekking in the mountains.

Pennsylvania: Lynn M. Moses was a school public librarian and is now a library advisor f the Pennsylvania Dept. of Education.

Rhode Island: Carin Steger Kaag is a libra at Lawnton E.S.

South Carolina: Tammy Williams is a Child Services Coordinator for Greenwood Cty. Lib She's loved to read ever since she can remem

South Dakota: LaVera Rose, Digital Libra at the South Dakota State Library, is a Sican Lakota from the Rosebud Reservation.

Tennessee: Karen McIntyre is a librarian at Westmeade E. S. in Nashville.

Texas: Jeanette Larson is a librarian for Aus Public Library. Although not a native, she's in Texas for 25 years.

Utah: Gabi Kupitz, a Brigham Young U. libra catalogs juvenile literature and special collect

Vermont: Grace Worcester Greene is Child Services Consultant for the VT Dept. of Libra

Virginia: Julie Dasso is a children's services ager with Fairfax Cty. Public Library. She ho dear spot in her heart for Texas, where she grev

Washington: Viki Ash-Geisler is a youth services coordinator for Spokane Public Lib

West Virginia: Sandra Myers Wiseman, a na of her state, is a school library media specialist Woodsdale E.S. and Ritchie E.S. in Wheelin

Wisconsin: Susan Awe, a native Cheesehea lives in Tijeras, NM, and works at the UNM as business librarian. She loves reading and rev ing for *Library Journal, Booklist,* and *Choice.*

Wyoming: Jill Rourke became a librarian because she loves finding just the right book just the right reader.

A Note from the Author/Illustrator

I LOVED THE IDEA OF WRITING AND ILLUSTRATING A BOOK about the United States, and I loved the process, too. My goal was to create something special, something truly unique. I hoped to stitch together America chronologically, from Delaware—the first state admitted to the Union—to Hawaii—the last state admitted. I was curious to see just how the country developed, how it actually *looked* at different periods of time.

I wanted each state's story to be written by a librarian from that state. That way, there would be 50 different voices to express some of the great diversity of our country. Librarians were the perfect choice because of my deep respect for them, because they have access to a lot of great reference books, and, most of all, because they are smart! I asked each librarian to explain why the place they call home decided so many years ago to become a state.

As an artist, my medium is quilts, or textile art. Quilt illustration is a perfect match for a book like this, not only because quilting is one of only two art forms that are uniquely American (jazz is the other), but because the United States came together much the way a quilt does—piece by piece.

I love my medium, and as a painter's palette contains all the colors of the rainbow, a quilter's palette contains all the colors of the rainbow *plus* tons of designs. Fabric is my palette, and I cannot begin to explain how much I enjoy it or how much fabric I own.

In this book, there is a unique piece of quilt art for each state. To speak to our country's rich history of folk art, I used motifs related to each state. When you turn to each state's page, I want there to be a special moment when the quilt strikes you as amusing or colorful or exciting.

I have thousands of pieces of fabric in my stash, containing hundreds of "conversational prints," which are fabrics that depict objects other than flowers. (Fabrics with flowers are called "florals.") In each illustration, there is a floral from The State Flower Collection, so each state flower is incorporated on the quilt for that state. The conversational prints I used depict artichokes, wheat, beets, and lots of other things I found to describe the important elements of each state. Believe me, not every state was easy!

One of my goals in the illustrations for the 50 states was never to repeat a fabric motif. That means every cow, ear of corn, and pig in this book is different. But I enjoyed going through piles of fabric to find the perfect pineapple or bird. And cows! You have to admit that we have a lot of cows in this country. Thank goodness there are a lot of fabric designers who love to draw them.

To work on a book about the United States may sound a bit daunting, and at times it was, but it also was a tremendous amount of fun.

—Adrienne Yorinks

Index